# HIGH SCHOOL SURVIVAL GUIDE

*Navigate Friendships, Ace School, Handle Peer Pressure, Stay Healthy, Build Confidence, Explore Careers, Prepare for the Future, and More!*

**TAYLOR MARR**

**Copyright 2024.**

**SPOTLIGHT MEDIA**

ISBN: 978-1-951806-57-6

For questions, please reach out to:

Support@ActivityWizo.com

**All Rights Reserved.**

No part of this book may be reproduced or transmitted in any form or by any means, electronic or mechanical, including photocopying, recording, or by any other form without written permission from the publisher.

# FREE BONUS

## SCAN TO GET OUR NEXT BOOK FOR FREE!

# Table of Contents

INTRODUCTION: .................................................................... 1

    THE PURPOSE OF THIS BOOK ........................................ 2

    HOW TO USE THIS GUIDE ............................................... 3

    SELF-COMPASSION AND PATIENCE ............................... 4

CHAPTER ONE: UNDERSTANDING THE HIGH SCHOOL JOURNEY ............................................................................. 7

    OVERVIEW OF HIGH SCHOOL LIFE ................................. 9

    EXPECTATIONS VS. REALITY ......................................... 11

    FINDING YOUR PLACE IN HIGH SCHOOL .................... 13

CHAPTER TWO: MAKING FRIENDS AND FOSTERING RELATIONSHIPS ................................................................... 17

    BUILDING HEALTHY FRIENDSHIPS ............................... 18

    DEALING WITH FRIENDSHIP CHALLENGES ................ 20

    NAVIGATING ROMANTIC RELATIONSHIPS ................. 23

    BUILDING POSITIVE RELATIONSHIPS WITH TEACHERS AND OTHER ADULTS ...................................................... 27

CHAPTER THREE: MAINTAINING HEALTH AND WELLNESS ............................................................................................. 31

    THE IMPORTANCE OF REGULAR EXERCISE ................ 32

    BALANCED DIET AND NUTRITION .............................. 34

THE IMPORTANCE OF SLEEP ..................................................... 36

BODY POSITIVITY AND SELF-LOVE ........................................ 38

CHAPTER FOUR: ORGANIZING FOR SUCCESS ....................... 41

TIME MANAGEMENT SKILLS ..................................................... 42

ORGANIZING YOUR SPACE FOR PRODUCTIVITY ............. 43

BALANCING SCHOOLWORK AND FREE TIME ................... 44

PRIORITIZING TASKS ................................................................. 46

CHAPTER FIVE: MASTERING EFFECTIVE STUDY HABITS ... 49

DEVELOPING STRONG STUDY SKILLS ................................. 50

STRATEGIES FOR NOTETAKING ............................................. 51

TEST PREPARATION TECHNIQUES ......................................... 52

UTILIZING SCHOOL RESOURCES ............................................ 54

CHAPTER SIX: MANAGING STRESS AND ANXIETY ............. 57

UNDERSTANDING STRESS AND ANXIETY ......................... 58

TECHNIQUES FOR MANAGING STRESS ............................... 59

SEEKING HELP WHEN NEEDED ............................................. 61

MINDFULNESS AND MEDITATION ....................................... 62

CHAPTER SEVEN: NAVIGATING PEER PRESSURE AND BULLYING ....................................................................................... 65

UNDERSTANDING PEER PRESSURE ........................................ 66

STRATEGIES FOR HANDLING PEER PRESSURE .................. 68

RECOGNIZING AND RESPONDING TO BULLYING ........... 69

BUILDING CONFIDENCE AND SELF-ESTEEM ..................... 70

CHAPTER EIGHT: PRIORITIZING MENTAL HEALTH ............. 73

RECOGNIZING SIGNS OF MENTAL HEALTH
CHALLENGES ......................................................................... 74

STRATEGIES FOR MAINTAINING MENTAL HEALTH ....... 75

WHEN TO SEEK HELP ................................................................ 76

REMOVING THE STIGMA AROUND MENTAL HEALTH .. 77

CHAPTER NINE: ACHIEVING ACADEMIC SUCCESS ............. 79

SETTING AND ACHIEVING GOALS ........................................ 80

DEVELOPING A POSITIVE ATTITUDE TOWARD
LEARNING .............................................................................. 81

GETTING GOOD GRADES: TIPS AND TRICKS ...................... 83

SEEKING EXTRA HELP: TUTORING AND ACADEMIC
RESOURCES ............................................................................ 84

CHAPTER TEN: PARTICIPATING IN EXTRACURRICULAR
ACTIVITIES .................................................................................. 87

BENEFITS OF EXTRACURRICULAR ACTIVITIES ................... 88

BALANCING SCHOOLWORK AND EXTRACURRICULARS
................................................................................................. 89

CHOOSING THE RIGHT ACTIVITIES FOR YOU ................... 91

LEADERSHIP OPPORTUNITIES IN SCHOOL ......................... 92

CHAPTER ELEVEN: EMBRACING INDIVIDUALITY AND DIVERSITY ................................................................................. 95

UNDERSTANDING AND RESPECTING DIFFERENCES ...... 96

THE IMPORTANCE OF INCLUSION ........................................ 97

ADVOCATING FOR YOURSELF AND OTHERS ..................... 98

NURTURING YOUR UNIQUE INTERESTS AND PASSIONS ................................................................................................... 99

CHAPTER TWELVE: DEVELOPING LIFE SKILLS .................... 101

BASIC FINANCIAL LITERACY ................................................ 102

SELF-CARE AND INDEPENDENCE SKILLS ......................... 105

COMMUNICATION AND CONFLICT RESOLUTION SKILLS ................................................................................................. 107

DECISION MAKING AND PROBLEM SOLVING SKILLS .. 109

CHAPTER THIRTEEN: PLANNING FOR THE FUTURE ......... 113

CAREER EXPLORATION AND PLANNING ......................... 114

COLLEGE PREPARATION: SAT, ACT, AND COLLEGE APPLICATIONS ......................................................................... 115

SCHOLARSHIPS AND FINANCIAL AID ............................... 118

VOCATIONAL PATHS: ALTERNATIVES TO COLLEGE .... 120

CHAPTER FOURTEEN: GRADUATION AND BEYOND ........ 123

REFLECTING ON THE HIGH SCHOOL JOURNEY .............. 124

PREPARING FOR THE TRANSITION ....................................... 125

EMBRACING CHANGE AND UNCERTAINTY ..................... 128

LIFELONG LEARNING: CONTINUING TO GROW BEYOND HIGH SCHOOL ........................................................................ 129

# CONCLUSION .............................................................................. 133

LOOKING BACK, LOOKING AHEAD ...................................... 134

EMBRACING YOUR UNIQUE JOURNEY ............................... 135

FINAL WORDS OF ENCOURAGEMENT ................................ 137

# INTRODUCTION:

# THE PURPOSE OF THIS BOOK

High school shouldn't be the best years of your life; there's too much to look forward to in later years. You'll have the chance to experience financial, emotional, and personal independence. There's also the joy that comes with being an adult who knows how to set and achieve goals while still going with the flow. If you're lucky, you might find a career you enjoy so much that it seems like play. In your free time, you'll be able to try new things and decide exactly how you want to spend your days.

However, you'll embrace freedom in ways you never expected in high school. You'll be able to do more things independently with friends, get your driver's license, and choose how you want to use your savings. Whether it's short-term goals like a vacation or long-term goals like saving for college, you'll be free to do much more than when you were younger.

That said, you can start preparing for the future right now regardless of whether you're in eighth grade, starting your freshman year, or about to become a junior. In this book, you'll learn fundamental ways to begin taking the wheel of your life. These techniques will set you on the path to success and happiness according to your own definition of what that might mean.

You might hear the word "growth" tossed around in your years as a high school student, but there is more to high school than meeting goals and personal development. There needs to be room for what makes you happy too. Finding a healthy balance is key.

Real growth isn't limited to your high school years by any stretch of the imagination. With that said, you can start developing healthy habits related to self-care, respect, inclusion, and independence by starting in high school.

The purpose of this book is to help you navigate the challenges of high school. Despite the daily grind of homework and classes, there are still amazing opportunities in high school that you won't find anywhere else.

While getting good grades is just one measure of success, high school is also a time when you should be learning about how to take care of yourself as an independent adult. Cooking, doing laundry, maintaining a car, keeping your room tidy, and nurturing friendships are just as important as getting good grades.

Of course, improving your academic standing is a great way to get a college admissions officer's attention or compete for a once-in-a-lifetime internship in your field of choice. In this book, you'll find solid tips on maintaining good grades while also capitalizing on all the "soft skills" you can learn during your high school years.

Additionally, this guide will help you take care of yourself physically and mentally. This means eating right when you can and knowing when to take a "mental health day" to reset from the demands of your everyday life.

# HOW TO USE THIS GUIDE

This guide can be read cover to cover, or you can pick and choose certain sections that interest you. It addresses most of the fundamental social dynamics and organizational skills you'll encounter in high school. Each section is written to stand alone, but there's plenty to gain from reading the whole book and making connections between topics. For example, Chapter 3 covers general health and wellness, but you can learn more about stress management in Chapter 6.

The best thing about this book is that it's yours. Unlike a scheduled class, this book is a compendium of topics you can pick up anytime, whenever you need it. Self-directed learning is a big indicator of your success in college or a future career. Your ability to follow a topic and determine which parts apply most to your life will serve you well. As you read, use what you can from each chapter, and don't worry too much about the rest.

# SELF-COMPASSION AND PATIENCE

Being compassionate with yourself is another key aspect of high school. Harvard researchers emphasize that practicing self-compassion is linked with better relationships and improved physical and mental health.

Your high school years will be among the busiest, most demanding years you'll ever experience. However, these years are also full of opportunities. High school will undoubtedly set you on a course for bigger and better things. On the way, be sure to treat yourself with respect and love. There's only so much you can do on any given day.

As you leave your early childhood years behind, remember what you loved to do as a kid and try taking up those habits again occasionally. Remember, growing up doesn't have to mean losing touch with your inner child and the things that once made you happy.

If high school seems overwhelming, ask yourself what will matter in two years or two decades. This doesn't mean you should fail French class because you won't use it, but you shouldn't panic if you don't get a perfect grade. Find the compassion to let yourself make some mistakes and carry on.

There's also a good deal to be said for patience. In fact, studies have shown that patient people experience much better mental health. You will have plenty of chances to practice patience in daily life, and the people who do often roll with the punches and maintain a more positive attitude than those who don't.

Not everything in high school will seem relevant at first, but it's all part of developing a good relationship with learning. Dive in deep when you feel motivated about a particular topic. You might find something there that will interest you for the rest of your life.

On the flip side, be patient with the stuff that doesn't hold your attention at first glance. High school is all about laying the groundwork for adulthood, and certain things you learn will come around again when you least expect it. Sure, you'll need math if you want to be an engineer, but you also might need it if you want to be a reporter or a musician. High school is all about the fundamentals. Stoke your thirst for learning now, and you'll be reaping the rewards for the rest of your life.

# CHAPTER ONE: UNDERSTANDING THE HIGH SCHOOL JOURNEY

When you look around your high school, a few of your fellow students might end up becoming your closest friends for life. This might be exhilarating to some people but terrifying to others. However, it's true that the new bonds you form in high school will be more intense and potentially last longer than any others you've formed up to this point in your life.

This isn't meant to scare or pressure you. The social aspect of high school happens on its own as you participate in classes and extracurriculars. You most likely also have existing friendships to maintain while you're meeting new people.

You'll find kids who are popular because they're kind to everyone and kids who only seem to form relationships based on fear or competitiveness. Meeting people with similar interests is far easier in high school when you have more freedom to choose your classes and join clubs.

In high school, grades begin to matter more for what you want to do with the rest of your life. Good grades aren't an absolute requirement for success, but they certainly help. While there are countless examples of cultural icons and business tycoons who did poorly in high school, remember that they are the exception and not the rule.

Research from Virginia Commonwealth University shows that people who attend school through at least 12th grade have higher life expectancy and earnings. It makes sense: the more education you have, the better access you have to higher-paying jobs. Those roles tend to come with opportunities to enjoy better food, safer housing, and comprehensive health care. So, while some days high school might seem like it's completely useless, you're still improving your future in concrete ways just by showing up and putting in an honest effort.

The major point of this book is to help you understand the challenges of high school more proactively so that you can tackle them with a clearer head. In that vein, the next sections of this guide will outline high school life, including what to expect from your day-to-day life and how to find your place as everything continues to change.

# OVERVIEW OF HIGH SCHOOL LIFE

Like most phases of school, high schools are divided into grade levels. In order, these are known as your freshman, sophomore, junior, and senior years. There are some schools that have a unique structure, but most follow the same four-year format.

High school is uniquely different compared to your time in elementary and middle school, namely for the level of independence you will be experiencing. While you're probably looking forward to these changes after hearing about them from others, keep in mind that you'll also have more responsibility.

For example, in most high schools, the workload will be significantly heavier compared to grammar school. This typically means more work throughout the day, but not all schools are heavy on homework that you need to do after hours. You may also have time to complete assignments during free periods like study hall.

To help you adjust to these increased demands on your time, you'll probably have a guidance counselor (or someone similar) available to assist you as needed. While this support system is in place at most high schools, you may need to set up an appointment or figure out when rotating personnel will be assigned to your school for the day.

You might even find that meetings and classes periodically shift online. For example, if your school district closes because of snow, you may still need to sign online and participate for the day. Platforms such as Schoology and PowerSchool make this possible. Many schools also maintain an online portal for students and their guardians to check grades throughout the marking period.

In addition to the increasing workload and responsibility of high school, there are still some major perks. You might have free periods when you're able to eat lunch, socialize, or catch up on work. In some towns, you can even leave campus during a free period once you turn 18.

There's also typically more freedom of choice in what you study. You'll be able to pick electives as you move into later grades that reflect your own personal interests, such as the arts, languages, and other topics.

Depending on your interests, you might need to look beyond your school's on-campus offerings. Some high schools, for instance, link up with local colleges and vocational-technical schools to allow students to attend classes there. If that sounds interesting, you can always ask your guidance counselor or peer support group.

You'll also likely have a broader choice of athletics and sports, like volleyball or rowing, that aren't offered in elementary and middle schools. There are also clubs and groups you can join based on your hobbies and interests.

Of course, these perks come with accountability, and you'll find that if you're late to class because of them, the school might take disciplinary action. Many high schools are pretty rigorous with attendance and discipline, and the consequences for breaking the rules can range from detention to outright suspension.

# EXPECTATIONS VS. REALITY

You might have been looking forward to high school as a chance to remake yourself, regain a little more control over your daily life, or find a new social group. In many cases, high school is indeed an opportunity to start fresh. However, you might notice that social nuances such as "cliques" are harder to overcome or break into than you might have expected.

Research has shown that the ideal high school size is about 500 students. It's ideal because it allows kids to have a variety of choices in courses and friend groups without being overwhelmed. In smaller schools, the diversity of available social groupings dwindles, and in larger ones, kids tend to get lost in a sea of faces. While you can and will change in high school, you might have to try harder to find friends and form connections based on the size of your school.

The important thing is to keep trying until you find what's healthy and fulfilling for you. High school is a place to make mistakes in relative safety before you leave home. It's a place to try new things or delve into your existing interests.

Above all, adopt a growth mindset toward failure. This means believing you can change and grow from your mistakes. Failure isn't a reflection of your personality or your worthiness; it's simply a way to develop a new aspect of yourself. This new aspect might be resilience or perseverance, two skills crucial to success and emotional well-being.

In fact, research defines adaptive resilience as what happens when you aim high, fail, and still attain more than you might have previously thought possible. There's nothing wrong with believing you can get into a good college or have your dream job. Although it might not pan out, the spark of trying might lead you farther than you would have gone otherwise. In high school, almost anything is possible, and it pays to have faith in that.

There are people who will tell you to bulk up your resume in one way or another because they believe that high school performance determines everything that comes afterward. While there may be a little truth to it, how you look "on paper" only carries you so far. You can have a stellar resume, but if you royally flunk an interview, you might not get into college or get that job you want. On the flip side, if you don't have the best grades, you can really impress a college admissions officer or employer with your interview.

High school is really a chance to solidify who you are and get to know yourself through experimentation and increased freedom of choice. Any good college admissions officer will still consider a student who doesn't have stellar grades on their transcript if they've pursued a range of passions, hobbies, interests, and/or extra knowledge outside the classroom. Remember that extracurriculars account for as much as 30 percent of your college application, and employers love to see them too.

According to the National Center of Education Statistics, there are currently 3,931 accredited institutions of higher learning in the United States alone. There are also tens of thousands of jobs, internships, and other ways to fill your gap year or start a career right after high school. The reality is that there's room for you to show off your skills without relying solely on your grades or your extracurriculars.

## FINDING YOUR PLACE IN HIGH SCHOOL

Experimenting with new things allows you to broaden your horizons and learn about different subjects. It's all too easy to get pigeonholed in high school, but don't let that stop you from following your interests, making connections, and meeting new people.

While friend groups are effective in making you feel like you belong and offering a social support structure, there are definite downsides. For example, cliques can be a cruel reality of high school life. Don't fall prey to the idea that you can't ever socialize with others in a positive way if you already belong to a friend group. Be the one who's accepting of everyone and open to new friendships.

Surprisingly, the most genuinely popular kids in high school are often those who live this way. Many kids who get along with everyone practice understanding and acceptance. They're not popular because they're "better." In fact, it's just the opposite. They're popular because they're secure in themselves and don't need to knock anyone else down.

While we'll explore cliques more deeply in the next chapter, for now, the idea is to get enthusiastic about the new things you'll be exposed to in high school. If you're afraid of trying new things, think about why that might be. Are you afraid of being rejected by a friend group? If that's the case, you might need to make a tricky, but ultimately healthy, transition to more authentic friendships.

If you're afraid of failing, you might need a new perspective on failure. It's not a strike against you but rather a way of evolving into a capable adult. In any case, look at your fears and try to shine a new light on them. Many problems in life can be solved simply by looking at them from a different angle.

It really is true that you don't know whether you'll be successful unless you try. Don't listen to the stereotypes. There are countless stories about so-called "theater nerds" trying a sport for the first time in high school and loving it. On the flip side, varsity athletes have tried out for the school musical and landed lead roles. Take advantage of the opportunities you have. Some schools have amazing chances for independent study, internships, and abroad programs.

The key is being open to trial and error. There's only so far logic can take you when you're trying to figure out what you like and who you are. For example, if you happen to love photography, that doesn't mean you'll be as enthusiastic about a drawing class.

High school is a bit of an open dare to try new things, learn to do what you want within reason, and be who you are without apology. In that spirit, take the opportunity to experiment with new electives, sports, and clubs. You might find you gain a new interest, career prospect, or friend group.

If you don't feel like you fit in anywhere, it's important to talk to someone about it. It's challenging to focus on your schoolwork or maintain your mental health if you don't feel like you belong. You might even try to overcompensate for not belonging by trying to be something you're not. These are negative trends that can have a long-term effect on your overall well-being. Talk to your parents, a school counselor, or even an independent therapist if things start to feel overwhelming. A trusted adult can help you figure out how to make the most of the situation and boost your confidence moving forward.

# CHAPTER TWO: MAKING FRIENDS AND FOSTERING RELATIONSHIPS

# BUILDING HEALTHY FRIENDSHIPS

Most people would agree that the friendships they made, or still maintain, from high school are some of the most important in their lives. This highlights the essential role that social connections play for kids in their teen years.

A significant part of forming lasting friendships is the willingness to resolve conflict and compromise. There will be conflict, as you can't have honesty and intimacy without it, but the ability to navigate through conflict together is the mark of a great friendship. According to researchers at Berkeley, this distinguishes friendships from peer acceptance.

Peer acceptance might make you popular and increase your feeling of belonging, but being accepted isn't the same as forming deeper connections. It's friendship that gets you through daily life with mutual caring and support. There is a popular saying that goes, "Every person needs just two friends." This is because that's all it takes to make a person feel like they have allies.

If you're relying on just a single person for validation and recognition, you might be putting a little too much pressure on that one relationship. It pays to put yourself out there and form new friendships. In terms of meeting people, there's a lot to be gained from habitual contact. When you're in blended settings that involve students from all grades, you might even realize the people you have the most in common with are in another grade.

You don't have to arrive at high school with an existing friend group. In fact, it's possible to build part of your social life on daily contact from regular classes or after-school clubs. Once you make friends, you might even form connections with their extended circle. Being open to meeting new people can broaden your system of friendships exponentially.

At the beginning of a friendship, think about the patterns you want to create. The general pattern of a relationship will often be established within the initial few days. If you bond together by gossiping at first, this might prove to be the main topic you have in common for the duration of your acquaintance. Therefore, if you don't like the direction your friendship is heading, say something. The other person might feel the same way.

While this might sound a little harsh, it does take some guts to realize your friendship isn't built on the right ideas. You'll find that the friends worth making will readjust to follow your lead at times. Similarly, you might have to be open to following their lead occasionally. This is all a way of saying it pays to find friends with true commonalities; friends you can discuss anything with without being hurtful to others.

It's also worth noting that common interests are a great way to form friendships. This might be old news to you, but it's good advice that bears repeating. Common interests can take you a long way past the superficial aspects of high school, beyond the cliques and the social pressures. If you have an interest you can develop in a club or a class, go for it. You might just meet your next great friend.

# DEALING WITH FRIENDSHIP CHALLENGES

Researchers at the University of Pittsburgh have reported that teens with strong relationships at home and at school are a whopping 66% less likely to have problems with mental illness or addiction. While it's no surprise that friendship is good for you, both mentally and physically, it would serve you well to broaden and deepen the connections in your social circle.

But what about when friendships are threatened? Sometimes, a friendship simply comes to an end; this often happens when the two of you grow apart. You might become more involved in music, while your childhood best friend becomes more interested in sports. You might not even have some huge falling out; you'll simply stop talking as often. Those people will just become part of your past and the mosaic of memories that make up a childhood.

You might find that many of your friendships shift like this as you enter and progress through high school. There's nothing wrong with growing out of a relationship. Neither of you can really do anything about it, especially if you're finding new friends who share your interests and personality.

Don't be alarmed if you find your social circle changing dramatically from one year to the next. While you don't necessarily want to make this a pattern for the rest of your life, during your teenage years, it's normal. It's part of figuring out who you are, what you find fulfilling, and how much you want to share with others.

On the other hand, you might find yourself dealing with friendships that don't seem healthy. The unhealthy aspect might be obvious, such as an old friend who starts to spend all their free time getting high. If that's not you, and it shouldn't be, then you need to think about ending that relationship. This doesn't mean shunning your friend right away, but if you want to help, you could try to intervene and see if your friend is willing to change before you completely cut ties.

If you're stressed about a risky connection, and you don't want to see an old friend get hurt, you should talk to an adult. This might be your parent, who can then talk to the friend's parent or a counselor at school. While talking to an adult is easier said than done, it's worth it for your own peace of mind to get over that roadblock and approach someone older who might have valuable perspectives on the situation. At the very least, you'll get your worries off your chest.

Some teens encounter this type of situation when one of their friends is suicidal. They worry about breaking their friend's trust by alerting an adult, but telling someone else is what's in that person's best interest. True friendship means dealing with hard issues and recognizing that your friends might not always know what they really need to get well.

Many teenagers who were suicidal later thanked the friend who intervened or warned an adult about what was going on. After they get help or go through therapy, these teens will almost always see clearer than before and recognize that others were only trying to do what was right. People who lose a loved one to suicide or drugs often say they wish they had done something. You might find you're helping someone stay alive by "betraying their trust."

However, no amount of trust is worth the price of death for either of you.

While these are extreme examples, you might find yourself navigating more common friendship challenges, such as dealing with peer pressure in a clique. These everyday problems can be just as stressful. Cliques are built on common behavior, and if you don't comply, you risk being shunned from the group.

The prospect of being shut out of a friend circle and having to start over can be daunting. Trying to find a new seat at lunch or meeting new people might feel deeply unfair and scary. This stress from your social group can spill over into other areas of your life and make it difficult to manage your schoolwork or other obligations.

Remember that no friendship is worth your emotional and mental health. In the short term, losing a friend or even an entire group of friends is painful, but you'll most likely end up meeting new people who fit into your life even better than the former group. While you recover from a falling out, take honest stock of who you are, what you enjoy doing, and what you want to do in the long term.

Some people jog to cope, while others like to go on car rides with their favorite music on. The possibilities are limitless. Some kids even cope by doing chores and working around the house, which can fit in nicely with long-term plans of becoming more independent after graduation.

We'll go into coping mechanisms in more depth in Chapter 6. For now, just trust that your high school years are all about getting to know yourself and identifying healthy habits and friendships that can last you a lifetime. If something doesn't feel right, it's probably not. Trust your gut, and above all else, protect your own right to peace of mind and act accordingly.

# NAVIGATING ROMANTIC RELATIONSHIPS

In high school, you're in a bigger mix of people than in middle school. You may even develop crushes and romantic interest in other students. If your feelings are reciprocated, that could lead to an ongoing relationship in high school.

Your first romantic relationship can set the course for subsequent relationships, including your behavior, what you expect, and what you get out of it. Since families don't typically talk about romantic relationships in detail, you might be left to take any insight you can get from pop culture or your friends.

On television, you'll often find unrealistic depictions of love as basically an obsession that blots out the characters' personalities. In stories, love is frequently shown as somehow undeniable and obvious, and it occurs like a lightning strike that lasts forever. However, researchers at Harvard have suggested that because people consume these depictions of romantic love without questioning them, they may be even more harmful than on-screen violence.

A failed first relationship, whether it just doesn't work out or it's abusive, can distort how you view romance going forward. It's important to be cautious and avoid rushing into anything. Of course, your first relationship could also go very well. You might have a lot of respect for one another, talk about all sorts of life issues, and resolve them together. You might not feel the pressure to be physical too early in your relationship. Keep in mind that there's time, and sometimes, the longer you wait, the better things go.

There are also plenty of high schoolers who don't date anyone in high school but later meet someone in college or while working their first job. It can happen when you're least expecting or looking for it. Instead, working on your own personality and interests while keeping an open mind can lead to unexpected connections.

According to Harvard researchers, teenagers are hungry for good information on romantic relationships. 27% of respondents in a national survey of older teens wanted more helpful information about starting a relationship, 36% needed advice to deal with breakups, and roughly a third wanted to know how to avoid getting hurt.

It's important to realize that relationship failures can give you as much insight as successes. What counts is that you process what happens, which might mean talking about it with a trusted friend, journaling about it, or even going to therapy.

What's tricky is that there are about as many definitions of love as there are people in love. It's all too easy to confuse love with infatuation or idolization. On the other hand, you might have deep feelings of respect and closeness for someone who isn't a romantic love interest. It may sound strange, but you can love someone without being "in love" with them.

There's a distinction between deep friendship and romantic love. As much as it might hurt to hear, you should appreciate the other person's honesty if they admit they don't love you in that way. After all, you wouldn't want your romantic partner making false statements of love just to try to keep you happy. The more you can help each other define your respective feelings, the happier you'll be in your relationship.

It also helps to consider the idea of love and talk about it with those who have experienced it. What does it feel like? You might find a startling distinction between infatuation, the all-encompassing excitement at the beginning of a relationship, and true love, which takes a much longer time to develop.

Love carries a component of comfort, contentment, and having found your "home" in another person. This may seem like the opposite of the initial infatuation you may experience when you're simply obsessed with spending time together. People with a healthy love can and do spend a surprising amount of time apart, whether at work, with friends, or just taking care of their own business.

It might also be useful to think about what love has meant across cultures and at different periods of time. The expectation of love in marriage is a relatively recent, and still not necessarily predominant, phenomenon. In many cultures and time periods, marriage was often a business agreement, or a way to make alliances, not a romantic institution. In fact, the "puppy love" that many teenagers experience was often looked down upon.

Of course, marriage itself is often no longer the goal. There is no correct definition of love. What remains the same, however, are the markers of healthy relationships. It always helps to consider the examples you see around you. Which adults in your life seem to be in healthy relationships?

A good romantic relationship can profoundly impact you in positive ways. It will make you respect yourself more because your romantic partner will see you on a deeper level and show you respect, which in turn impacts how you see yourself. It can also give you hope and inspire you to be caring and generous.

On the other hand, if you're often worried or depressed about a relationship, it's time for a change. This might involve resolving issues with your partner or ending things and moving on. If you decide to work on your flaws, how do you get to the point of having a healthy romantic relationship? There are concrete things to aspire to, like honesty, effective communication, solving problems together, managing anger, and forgiveness.

Adults in healthy relationships value and seek out each other's opinions, often exploring what it takes to build and maintain a mature relationship. They might specifically point out that they like their partner's communication style or how they demonstrate respect for each other's insights. They might encourage each other to pursue outside interests and friendships or get physically fit to meet their long-term health goals. While some of these are specific to lifelong partnerships, the point is that it can help to think about what you ultimately want out of a romantic relationship.

Now, a word about safe sex. You'll find that, if nothing else, it's important for your peace of mind to engage in protected sex. This means condoms, for certain, and possibly birth control. Birth control will help prevent an unplanned pregnancy, but only condoms can prevent disease. Although many sexually transmitted infections (STIs) can be treated, it doesn't make them less difficult to deal with. Going to a doctor's office or Planned Parenthood to get tested might be enough to scare you off unprotected sex.

Then there's the fact that treatment can involve pricey drugs you'll have to take for weeks at a time while avoiding sexual contact with anyone else. The most serious STIs, such as HIV, don't have a known cure. HIV treatment, in particular, requires patients to take medications for the rest of their lives. Some of those drugs compromise organ health but extend a patient's overall lifespan. Don't let anyone tell you that every STI is completely curable and easy to treat in the interest of having unprotected sex.

STIs aside, save sex for someone with whom you share trust and emotional intimacy. There's no big hurry; you can have physical fun in lots of ways without actually having sex. You should also wait to be physically intimate with someone who will be honest about their own sexual activity and their true feelings for you. Ideally, wait until you're in a stable, exclusive relationship and you've both been tested or talked openly about having sex for the first time. As with so many aspects of a good relationship, open communication is key.

# BUILDING POSITIVE RELATIONSHIPS WITH TEACHERS AND OTHER ADULTS

During your high school years, you'll encounter a range of adults: teachers, coaches, counselors, and bosses, to name a few. Without a doubt, you'll find people you admire in the mix. This may be due to the way they talk to you. For example, you might find yourself full of new respect for a math teacher simply because they treat you like your opinions matter.

There are endless lessons to be learned from adults you admire. If you have a positive relationship with your parents, guardians, or close relatives, then you might find it easier to interact with adults. There's a lot to be said for keeping open communication with the trusted adults in your life. This might be the parent of one of your friends or a neighbor you've known since you were young. These adults often have your best interest in mind as the companion of their children or someone who's often in their household.

It's been shown that this type of link between a teenager and a trusted adult outside the family can be key for your emotional and physical health as you navigate high school. While it's not an ideal situation, there may be things you aren't comfortable talking about with your own parents or guardians and would rather talk about with another adult. It's best to try to solve certain problems with adult help rather than going without help at all.

Some high schoolers think about a certain household as a welcoming place to hang out, especially if they don't feel accepted in their own homes. It's wonderful to find adults other than your parents or guardians who appreciate who you are as a person, but make sure you're showing respect for them as well. If your mom is friends with your friend's mom, it could put your friend's mom in an awkward situation if you only want to vent about family disagreements.

By the same token, be aware of your own boundaries and when they're being crossed. Don't stand for any adult talking to you in an unwelcome or inappropriate manner. The power differential in a friendship between a teenager and an adult is real, and age plays a significant role. A 15-year-old talking with a 30-year-old is not the same as a 17-year-old talking to an 18-year-old, even though both involve a minor and an adult.

Age differences are a massive component of relationships when you're younger, mainly because you're changing so rapidly at a young age. You might not even have access to certain freedoms, such as driving or buying alcohol. These are things an adult can manipulate. Keep this in mind when relating to adults, even if they're only legal adults who've recently turned 18 and still go to your high school.

You have the right to feel safe with the adults you meet. If something happens that makes you uncomfortable, get some distance. If that doesn't work, or if the problem is serious, go to a trusted adult for help. Your first responsibility is to protect yourself and set healthy boundaries.

# CHAPTER THREE: MAINTAINING HEALTH AND WELLNESS

# THE IMPORTANCE OF REGULAR EXERCISE

As you've likely heard before, regular exercise greatly improves your physical and mental health. If you're not on a team sport at school, you might find yourself lacking in exercise and feeling sluggish or unmotivated. Exercise is about more than just maintaining a healthy weight. People of all sizes get into exercise and feel amazing benefits, regardless of what it does for their weight.

When you don't stress your system positively with some exercise or feel what it's like to get physically tired, your body tends to fall into a state of maintenance fatigue. You get used to using less energy and never enjoy the thrill of a good sweat and sore muscles. Without exercise, you never get the release of endorphins that accompany intense exercise, and you don't get to enjoy the state of relaxed focus that comes after as the body's natural reward.

Experts at the Mayo Clinic endorse exercise for teens to build bone and muscle strength, two things that can affect your quality of life for decades to come. For example, loss of bone density due to inactivity is a major source of health problems for older women. A high-impact workout like jogging can help prevent such problems.

Of course, you need to find some form of exercise that not only suits you but that you enjoy. If you don't like cardio, which is a highly repetitive form of exercise, you could try mixing it up with something like interval training. Only 20 minutes of alternating a minute of sprints with a minute of walking has been shown to be a more effective form of building muscle than steady-state jogging alone.

If you don't want to hit the streets in sneakers, there are plenty of high-impact interval training workouts free on YouTube. You might find these less intimidating than they sound while also being more effective. Plus, every step counts regardless of how you get it. For example, walking to school is one way to incorporate exercise into your schedule without having to set aside extra time. You'll find that the physical effort and fresh air do you enormous good.

You can also tie exercise into a hobby or interest. It's easy enough to imagine combining a love of photography with hiking, but what about underwater photography and swimming? If you're in an urban area, there are neighborhoods to explore on foot for amazing photos, or you can walk your dog to bond with your pet. If you're the kind of person who doesn't enjoy team or social sports, you might still love spoiling your dog with a trip around the neighborhood.

In addition to having stellar benefits for physical health, there are also mental benefits that'll set you up for a better life in your adult years. Overall, exercise is an effective way to head off depression and promote healthier sleep.

If you feel like you're getting less exercise than you should, you're in good company. Researchers have found that only 24% of kids aged 6 to 17 are getting the recommended hour of physical activity a day. This recommended amount of time spent exercising will only lessen as you get older. In your adult years, exercising 30 minutes a day is more than sufficient to achieve and maintain optimal health. Don't be put off by the numbers. Any physical activity you partake in is a step in the right direction. Skateboarding, playing fetch with the dog, and doing chores all count.

# BALANCED DIET AND NUTRITION

Good nutrition goes hand in hand with exercise because you need to fuel your body throughout the day and feed it well for your muscles to recover effectively. This specifically means eating a protein-rich meal or a snack within a half hour after a workout. With proper nutrition, you'll find your body will start to feel stronger and more balanced, even if you don't see a change on the scale. Muscle is denser than fat, so you might be the same weight but look different in your body composition.

As a teenager, you're at a crucial stage of physical development. Curating good eating habits now can lead to lifelong health. Forget counting calories, and instead, focus on eating when you're hungry and not overeating to the point of discomfort. Your body will tell you how much is enough and when it needs food.

It's also key to think about the content of what you eat. It's fine to splurge and eat junk occasionally, such as a bag of Doritos or a pint of ice cream. However, if you find yourself eating junk food because you're bored, sad, or emotional, that can be a slippery slope to developing an unhealthy relationship with food.

It helps to see food as fuel and to pay attention to how you feel *after* you eat. If you don't feel rejuvenated, your body is probably trying to tell you that you need better nutrients to fuel yourself. It pays off to understand the macros of a good diet and the proper balance of proteins, fats, and carbohydrates.

> **Basic healthy proteins include** chicken, yogurt, beans, nuts, and nut butters. Watch out for additives and sweeteners, as too much sugar can make things like yogurt and peanut butter unhealthy.
>
> **Sources of healthy fats include** avocados, seeds like chia and flax, nuts and nut butters, certain cheeses, full-fat yogurt, olive oil, and fish like salmon. Don't be afraid of fats; your brain is composed of fat and needs good fat to function optimally!
>
> **Healthy carbohydrates include** fruits and vegetables, as well as whole-grain bread and oatmeal.

As a rule, aim to avoid processed foods like the ones in the frozen aisle and most packaged snack foods. Steer clear of sugar and excessive salt, except for the occasional treat. It can feel like deprivation at first, but you will see that your body learns to enjoy and even crave wholesome foods like fresh fruit instead of soda.

You'd be surprised at the number of delicious dishes you can make with wholesome ingredients. Try looking online for health recipes or check out blogs by people experimenting with making tasty, nutrient-rich foods.

In general, school lunches aren't the best as far as nutrition and even taste. If you can, packing your lunch gives you the ability to control what you eat at school. Cheap ramen is simple to make and cooks up into something gourmet and healthy when you add lean meat, peas, broccoli, baby Bok choy, carrots, or any of your other favorite vegetables. Skip the high-sodium flavor packet and use beef or chicken broth instead.

Learning to cook a handful of healthy, tasty, and economical meals like this while you're still in high school will see you right through college or your first job. If you focus on the macros of a good diet, you'll be getting essential vitamins, minerals, and antioxidants that all maintain your immune system, enhance your brain's functioning, and promote overall well-being.

Eating for good health can be tough at first. Cutting sugar is no easy task, especially if you've grown up eating a lot of it. Your teenage years are the first time when you must take control of what you eat. For example, once you can drive and start earning money for chores or with a part-time job, what you buy at the grocery store is up to you.

That's when it's key to treat your body right. Your body learns to do without a lot of sugar, salt, and processed foods. The reward of feeling energetic, strong, clear-headed, and calm will ultimately convince you it's the path to take. Give it some time, and don't give up.

# THE IMPORTANCE OF SLEEP

Sleep is key to health. You might notice this in obvious ways, such as when you feel nauseated the next day from pulling an all-nighter. Sleep deprivation can also manifest in more insidious ways, such as irritability and lack of focus.

If possible, try to establish a regular sleep schedule with a predictable routine. When you go to bed and wake up can be as important as the amount of sleep you get. For example, you're not going to feel as well-rested if you go to bed one night at 2 a.m. and wake at 10 a.m. even though you still had 8 hours of sleep. That's because your body's circadian rhythm naturally works on a schedule.

No one's going to fault you for staying up late occasionally or sleeping in on the weekends, but good sleep hygiene involves a solid schedule that you stick to most nights. As with diet and exercise, perfection is never the goal since that's unrealistic. Simply aim for the best you can do and enjoy the times when you don't hit the goal.

There are some specific things you can do to build a solid sleep schedule. Start by making your bedroom quiet, comfortable, and dark. This might require blackout shades or heavy curtains, depending on how many windows you have in your room. Darkness is important for your circadian rhythm and to get recuperative rest at night. Although quiet is important, blocking out other household or environmental noises with white noise is a great method of getting better quality sleep. In fact, there are plenty of free apps for white noise.

If you can, avoid electronic devices an hour before you go to sleep. Blue light sends wake-up signals to your brain instead of the winding-down cues you need near bedtime. The same goes for eating any kind of large meal. If you can avoid eating an hour or more before you fall asleep, you'll find you sleep better and wake up feeling more rested.

Sleep is often one of the first things your doctor will ask you about when you mention any symptoms because good sleep is the marker of a healthy body. Do yourself a favor and protect your sleep with some of the tips here. You'll find it pays off in a million ways.

On the other hand, if you find you're sleeping too much, this can be an indicator of depression or some other health problem. The definition of too much sleep is arbitrary, but if you're taking multiple naps a day and sleeping for hours at a time, you should consider seeing a doctor. This is especially true if you don't feel rested afterward, regardless of how much you slept.

Talk to your parents or guardians about seeing a doctor if you experience any major changes in your sleep patterns. It might help treat any health conditions if you identify them earlier rather than later.

# BODY POSITIVITY AND SELF-LOVE

High school is a time of great personal development and growth. You might find you're shedding certain aspects of your personality as quickly as you're gaining others. At this age, you're changing physically, mentally, and emotionally while simultaneously being exposed to others who are going through the same thing.

What's most important is to not lose sight of who you really are, even if you're uncertain and exploring your personal identity now. Questioning who you are is valuable personality development; putting your feelings down on paper can be a helpful way to gauge what's going on in your life. This can be done through writing in a journal, painting, taking photographs, or just doodling.

Remember, always keep your essential uniqueness in mind. Emphasize your strengths rather than negatively comparing yourself to others. In fact, even when evaluating your strengths, it never pays to compare yourself to others. Focus on what makes you feel good by itself, not because you're getting external validation and compliments. In other words, focus on the process, not the product.

For instance, think about how good jogging or playing the guitar makes you feel instead of chasing a narrow goal of getting skinnier or being as famous as a rockstar. Lofty goals are important and can be motivating, but there's no sense in working towards a long-term goal if you don't enjoy the process.

American society is growing more supportive of individualism and recognizing that the idea of "normal" isn't the same for everyone. It's always a worthy goal to accept yourself and, above all, not beat yourself up due to supposed "negatives." While you should acknowledge your mistakes, there's no point beating yourself up about perceived failures on the way to improvement.

Take a moment to think about the people around you. Do your friends emphasize the positives and the process of personal development, or are they more obsessed with accolades and looking good to others? You shouldn't necessarily dump your friend group and search for another if they fall into the latter category, but you might consider how you fit into the equation and figure out ways to encourage uniqueness in your social circle.

# CHAPTER FOUR: ORGANIZING FOR SUCCESS

# TIME MANAGEMENT SKILLS

Once you reach high school, you're likely to have more responsibilities and commitments than ever. This includes academics, extracurriculars, and personal pursuits. It's important to build a foundation of organizational skills so that you finish what needs to be done on time.

One of the first things you can focus on is developing concrete time-management skills. The first step is to set goals, which is an essential life skill. To be effective, goals should be clear, have a timeframe or deadline, and, above all, be realistic. It's useless to set a goal of reading a 200-page novel in one evening because you'll never succeed. A more useful goal would be reading 25 pages a night for eight nights.

You also need to learn how to prioritize, such as listing tasks according to urgency and importance. This will give you a sense of control over what needs to be done. Don't underestimate the emotional and motivational components of planning ahead, as big, urgent goals can be daunting. Plenty of people make a list of major priorities but then end up procrastinating simply because they don't know how to begin tackling them.

It can pay off to complete some small tasks before a major one to build a sense of momentum. Once you've taken care of a few easy tasks, such as emptying your garbage, writing a quick email to your teacher, or putting fresh paper into your binder, you'll have a sense of accomplishment that you can build on. Starting that essay might not seem like such a daunting task after that.

There are countless planners and apps to break down your schedule into manageable pieces. You can keep it simple or get as involved and detailed as you want. Some people even make planners an art form. There's absolutely no difference, however, between a gorgeous planner and a scribbled outline on a scrap of paper. What's important is that you're thinking about your schedule, planning, and noting things down.

You might find you even get more done by writing down a schedule. Even if you don't follow it word-for-word, it will remain in the back of your head, guiding what you do. You might surprise yourself when you go back to a schedule you've written up and realize how closely you've stuck to it, even if you weren't referring to it constantly over the course of the day.

## ORGANIZING YOUR SPACE FOR PRODUCTIVITY

Having a tidy surface with space to work is always a good jumpstart to any project. Organize your books, materials, and supplies, and get rid of anything extraneous on your desk. A helpful method is to create designated spaces in your room for different activities. You might have a desk or table with space for textbooks, your computer for studying, and a group of pillows on the corner of your bed for reading. You can devote a separate corner of your room to houseplants, a shelf for board games, or a space for sneakers. You'd be surprised how many different "microcosms" you can create in your room.

When setting up your workspace for studying, think about ergonomics and your posture when you sit at your desk. Position the chair armrests so that your computer keyboard is a little lower than your elbows. If possible, have an external monitor for a laptop. Ideally, you should be looking forward at the external monitor screen instead of down at your laptop. While this isn't always possible, it can make a big difference if you have hours of computer work ahead of you. There's nothing worse than facing a tight deadline with your neck and back already stiff from a poor desk setup.

It also pays to organize your supplies and necessities with shelves, bins, or paper files. Label these clearly and keep them in view. At the very least, have one bin or section of your desk devoted to completed paperwork to ensure you bring all your finished assignments to school. Even if most of your assignments are digital, keeping some basic office supplies on hand will save you the irritation of looking for what you need when you're already short on time.

# BALANCING SCHOOLWORK AND FREE TIME

One of the most useful things you can do to manage your time is to create a routine. This routine might be a little different each day, but the key aspect is that you're allocating specific slots of time for schoolwork and free time.

Maybe you always have a study hall after math to finish your assignment while the lesson's fresh, freeing you up after school to paint a mural at the community center. Maybe most of your assignments have a due date of Thursday or Friday, making Wednesday crunch time. Try to free up time by allocating extra time to meet a deadline or two earlier in the week. This way, you might have time to watch your favorite series with your best friend on Thursday evening.

You can also include weekends into the mix. Some students wake up on Saturday morning to complete their homework as early as possible, freeing up the rest of their weekend for sports and relaxation time. There's plenty to be said for this philosophy of "getting ahead of the game."

Maintaining consistency like this helps you build good study habits. Nothing's more stressful than feeling like you're out of time or you don't have enough time to finish what you need to do. If you nip that stress in the bud by jumpstarting your weekly assignments, you'll find that you have more breathing room later in the week to complete work more efficiently and with better recall.

Of course, it's also important to have downtime. It's worth scheduling these in to ensure you don't skip over breaks. Keep your schoolwork in check and your personal well-being in mind, as prioritizing and planning play big roles here. If you know social studies homework takes you the most time, consider finishing it first to get a big chunk of your schoolwork out of the way early in the week. If you know you must get a B or better in algebra this quarter to get into advanced placement chemistry next year, focus on that schoolwork first when your mind is freshest.

You can mix things up for the sake of variety. Complete an easy, quick assignment first to get one in the bag and build momentum, then take on a tricky assignment, followed by another straightforward task. Before long, you'll be cruising through homework.

The idea is to avoid last-minute cramming, which really doesn't do anything for long-term recall. Cramming can allow you to regurgitate a lot of information onto a test page the next day, but your brain will then promptly forget most of what you put into it. This makes it ineffective for long-term retention if you take classes that build on each other over time.

## PRIORITIZING TASKS

The first step in prioritizing tasks is to assess importance and urgency. If you have different tasks on your plate, look at which ones are most important or have the shortest deadlines. Consider critical deadlines and set them at the top of your list. The crucial thing is to keep the deadlines on your radar so that you don't get behind.

There are other prioritization methods you might be interested in looking into as well. The Eisenhower Matrix and the ABC method are two popular models. They're handy when you feel overwhelmed by a great number of assignments, and you just need to get a good overview before you dive in.

It also helps to break down big projects into more manageable pieces. Large projects demand significant time and effort. Plan on completing smaller subtasks of a project and prioritizing them with your other assignments. You might need to write two pages of a five-page paper on Monday to get the assignment under control for a deadline next Tuesday.

This type of working style allows you to make progress consistently, feel good about it, and keep from getting overwhelmed. It always feels better to be ahead of the game or on target with deadlines. This type of skill is also highly valued in the working world, where it's known as "working backward from deadlines."

# CHAPTER FIVE: MASTERING EFFECTIVE STUDY HABITS

# DEVELOPING STRONG STUDY SKILLS

Building good study habits is a cornerstone of academic success. Some kids seem to cruise by without studying much, but they might be underestimating how much studying time they're really putting in. They might also be brilliant outliers who aren't really challenged by high school. In either case, anyone can benefit from learning how to study more effectively.

If you employ solid study techniques, use effective notetaking strategies, implement proven test-prep techniques, and take advantage of your school's resources, you're bound to optimize your learning to reach your academic goals. One of the key factors is time management. It pays to make a study schedule and integrate it into your daily routine. For example, you might study the most efficiently right after tennis practice, or you might need to eat dinner before hitting the books. Try out strategies and schedules to see what works for you.

Once you start studying, a popular tactic is practicing self-explanation, which simply involves verbalizing concepts to yourself out loud or on paper. You'll find that stretching your brain to rephrase concepts and lessons like this goes a long way toward reinforcing comprehension. Next, engage in what's called retrieval practice. This means testing yourself on a regular basis to keep your memory of concepts as fresh as possible.

Another proven technique is to teach others. Explaining concepts to your friends, classmates, or even family members can solidify your own comprehension. If you regularly study with a partner, break up the concepts into two groups so that each of you can learn half of them and teach them to the other.

Don't forget to pay attention to your environment while you're studying. We covered organization in the last chapter, but this goes above and beyond organization. For one thing, you'll need to minimize distractions. Even the most organized desk is useless if your phone is going off every 15 seconds. Minimize interruptions to enhance your focus on what's important.

You'll also want to make sure you have good lighting and a comfortable chair or study area. You don't want to be combating eye or neck strain when you're on deadline for a French class assignment.

## STRATEGIES FOR NOTETAKING

Better notetaking techniques can vastly improve your studying time. For one thing, make sure you're actively listening during class. Find the main ideas, key concepts, and critical examples in the teacher's lesson plan. It always helps to ask questions, which can clarify misunderstandings and enhance comprehension and retention.

As far as your actual notes go, there are two methods for structured note-taking that you might want to try. The Cornell Method involves dividing your note paper up into three sections: one for main ideas, one for supporting details, and a final for summarization. This type of visual highlighting and delineating of the most important concepts might help you recall your notes verbatim in your mind's eye.

Mind-mapping is another technique that involves making diagrams to connect different concepts to facilitate comprehension and recall. It's a bit too complicated to go into here, but if you are a visual learner, you might want to look up an example to see how it's done.

It's also essential to organize your notes well. This means using headings and subheadings to place notes into specific sections based on subject matter. Highlighting key points with a highlighter or sticky tab can help emphasize the most important information and make it easier to see crucial concepts quickly and efficiently during review.

Another strategy is using symbols and abbreviations to save yourself a bit of writing. Notetaking in class might be easier if you create your own system to mark out which topics you'll need to study later.

## TEST PREPARATION TECHNIQUES

One of the major ways of effectively preparing for a test is reviewing and summarizing. You won't be able to get past a looming test without looking back at your notes. It helps if you do this regularly before the test is even scheduled. Set aside time once or twice a week to review the previous week's material.

Consistently revisiting class material like this will reinforce comprehension and retention over time.

As far as summarizing goes, you're in control of rephrasing key concepts, condensing complex topics, and coming up with concise summaries that make sense to you. The process of summarizing may be beneficial for remembering important information. This is particularly effective when studying for written essay exams.

Another method involves making flashcards with questions or key points on one side and answers on the other so that you can quiz yourself later. Alternatively, there are apps for that if you'd rather study on the go or use your phone instead of your laptop. You can find free ones if you spend a little time looking.

For technical subjects, doing practice problems with an answer key can help you learn how to use formulas and complete similar problems. You're probably familiar with this from math homework, but you can apply it to just about any problem-based assignment. Engaging in problem-solving this way reinforces comprehension and the process of arriving at the correct answer.

Taking full advantage of study resources will help you go a long way. While you've got your textbooks, which often have more study problems than you'll be assigned, you can also take advantage of online resources. When you have a test coming up, try seeking out educational platforms and websites. There are a ton set up to supplement learning and provide additional insights beyond what you might have been exposed to in the classroom.

Try searching for a topic in connection with "microlearning," a trendy way of teaching employees around the world. You might come across some snappy, bite-sized lessons that are relevant to what you're studying in school.

Another great way to challenge yourself is to form a study group. You can always find other people willing to collaborate to discuss concepts, share knowledge, and clarify questions when a test is coming up. Two heads are better than one, and five are even better. If you don't feel comfortable meeting outside of school, see if one of your teachers will allow you to come early or stay late.

## UTILIZING SCHOOL RESOURCES

Don't forget that your school should be there to help you with all of this. High schools often have libraries with a range of books and resources to broaden your comprehension of various subjects. There will also be some kind of study space, whether it's in the library itself or in designated study cubicles.

Many high schools also often provide tutoring and academic support. This might mean a peer tutoring program where students who have passed classes, or performed at a high-level, help classmates with challenging subjects.

You can also go directly to your teacher for help. Teachers want to see you succeed, and most of them are eager to help. It's their chosen profession, after all. Seek teachers out during office hours, if that's how your school does it, or catch them after class to see if they can help.

Some schools go above and beyond by organizing study skills workshops. Consider yourself lucky if your high school is one of them. An in-person workshop with a trained or experienced leader is worth the hours of time you would normally spend at home alone searching for resources on the internet.

Mastering effective study habits is pretty much the foundation of academic success, regardless of how smart you are. If you develop good study skills in high school, use effective notetaking strategies, and take advantage of your school's resources, you'll optimize your academic experience and set yourself up for success for years to come.

# CHAPTER SIX: MANAGING STRESS AND ANXIETY

# UNDERSTANDING STRESS AND ANXIETY

Stress can occur when you're faced with a challenging task, an upsetting situation, or too many demands. Eustress is the positive type of stress that can motivate you to work hard or push you to step outside your comfort zone. Distress, on the other hand, is a negative form of stress that results in anxiety.

When you're anxious, you most likely feel overwhelmed by the stressors in your life. Symptoms of anxiety often include a fast heartbeat, difficulty sleeping, and trouble concentrating. In some cases, anxiety is a temporary reaction that makes sense in a particular set of circumstances. If you're worried for a few days about an upcoming exam, that's perfectly natural and understandable.

However, there are also times when anxiety spirals out of control, and you start to feel excessively nervous. When that happens, it's important to recognize when you need coping mechanisms or help from others to reduce stress in your daily life. Make sure the coping mechanisms you choose are positive and healthy.

Although you might see your peers experimenting with drugs or alcohol to manage stress, turning to substances or other unhealthy habits will only make you feel worse in the long run. For example, even if smoking marijuana or using tobacco at a high school age is legal in some states, it's still a terrible idea to expose your brain to these substances while you're learning and growing.

The Mayo Clinic reports that teens and young adults who use marijuana are at a higher risk of abnormal brain development and impaired coordination, memory, and judgment. This means you could be jeopardizing your ability to remember important details from class or make solid decisions about how to approach a major project.

## TECHNIQUES FOR MANAGING STRESS

Ultimately, it's up to you to determine which stress management techniques are most effective. This might take some trial and error as you figure out exactly what puts you more at ease. For instance, your friends might feel rejuvenated after a night on the couch, while you prefer to be more active when you're recovering from a stressful day.

Stress is cumulative, so it may take a prolonged effort to manage your stress successfully. Some common techniques to eliminate stress and mentally reset include the following:

- Going for a walk
- Taking a bath
- Working on a hobby
- Talking it out with friends or loved ones
- Playing with pets
- Watching a favorite movie or TV show
- Journaling, writing, or drawing

Besides individual actions like going for a jog, you should also consider whether you need to adjust your lifestyle to reduce stress. When you're struggling to balance school, work, and free time, it's important to know when you're at your limit. Saying "no" to further demands on your time is a healthy way to protect your own mental health and ensure you don't go overboard on commitments.

You should aim to feel in control of your day-to-day schedule. You can't decide when school starts or whether you must work certain hours, but you can make other choices that affect how well you manage those obligations. For example, if you know you have a big test on Monday, it's probably a good idea to leave part of your weekend free to study. This will give you enough time to prepare without panicking at the last minute and creating stress about your grades.

It's also important to take breaks. Forcing yourself to push through even if you're tired will only cause you to burn out faster. When you're doing something stressful, schedule short breaks to decompress and mentally reset. This could be as simple as taking a quick nap or playing a video game for 15 minutes in between chores or your schoolwork.

If you're facing a long-term challenge, such as applying to colleges or training for sports tryouts, make sure to take days off occasionally. Relaxing will help you refill your tank and refocus. When you're calmer and refreshed, you'll be able to see the situation more clearly and get back to work with a renewed sense of motivation.

# SEEKING HELP
# WHEN NEEDED

Some amount of stress is normal, but you may experience times when your stress levels are out of control. When this happens, your normal techniques and coping mechanisms are unlikely to be effective. Instead, it might be time to seek out additional help and support.

A trusted adult, such as a parent, guardian, coach, or neighbor, can listen to your concerns and provide advice about the best way to proceed. Sometimes, just having another person's input and perspective can lessen the impact of stress because you know someone else is on your side. Confiding in a trusted adult to help guide you through a stressful situation can be invaluable, especially if you have limited experience with the situation. For example, if you accidentally lose your driver's license, you might not know what to do because you're still a new driver.

With more familiar problems, your friends, siblings, or classmates may be able to help as well. If you're having trouble with a particular subject, there's nothing wrong with asking someone to study with you or review key topics. You can even tutor each other in your strong areas, which makes for a more balanced exchange.

If none of these suggestions seem viable, it could be time to seek professional help. Most schools have guidance counselors available for exactly this reason. Even if you don't want to talk to a school counselor, they likely have other resources they can recommend in your local area. Telehealth has also made it easier than ever to find therapists with flexible hours and a range of different specialties.

Instead of going to a physical office to speak with someone, you can set up an appointment by phone or video chat. This way, you can stay where you're comfortable and avoid the hassle of driving somewhere new. Remote appointments may also be a better fit if you're nervous about talking with a counselor face-to-face.

Don't wait until you feel like you're at your mental or emotional limit to ask for help. If your daily life is too stressful to manage on your own, that's unlikely to change without making significant changes to your habits, routines, or obligations. Working through the problem with a neutral third party can help you gain perspective on the situation and see where you can scale back in some aspects of your life.

# MINDFULNESS AND MEDITATION

Mindfulness is a form of meditation that emphasizes being aware of what you're feeling, thinking, and experiencing. The goal isn't to apply judgments or react to what you notice about your innermost thoughts. Instead, it's about accepting who you are and understanding that complicated emotions are part of everyday life.

Over time, mindfulness has expanded to include a more general form that takes place outside of traditional meditation. This approach reinforces being completely in the present rather than dwelling on the past or stressing about the future. Being mindful is about letting go of past mistakes instead of constantly revisiting embarrassing moments or worrying about potential obstacles in the future.

When you have an unpleasant thought or a judgment about what's happening, acknowledge and let go of it. Remember, the purpose of mindfulness isn't to stop yourself from having those thoughts; it's about limiting your reaction instead of allowing your thoughts to overwhelm you. As you work through the underlying causes of your emotions, you'll have a better understanding of why you feel the way you do in response to different experiences.

You can also pursue other types of meditation using techniques such as focusing on your breathing, concentrating on a particular problem, or repeating a mantra. If you're new to meditation, there are guided options available online where you can follow along with an instructor. Meditation has many different forms, so you can choose whether you prefer to lie down, sit, or move.

Meditation is a healthy addition to any stress-management routine. If you decide to meditate on a regular basis, consider setting aside a special time only for meditation. Some people enjoy meditating in the morning to get ready for the coming day, while others meditate at night to calm themselves before sleep. You can even set up a designated area with pillows and soothing music to create the right environment.

# CHAPTER SEVEN: NAVIGATING PEER PRESSURE AND BULLYING

# UNDERSTANDING PEER PRESSURE

Keeping an open mind when it comes to forming friendships is one of the best things you can do for yourself in high school. Some people who meet in high school go on to start businesses, get married, or move to the same college together as roommates. Be open to what other people bring to the table. Don't buy into the idea that everyone must stick to a certain social clique and be defined by it. Instead, let people surprise you.

Of course, some people find it easier to start conversations and ignite new friendships than others. But even this can change in high school, and it might happen almost overnight. You might find it easier to strike up conversations when you have things in common, like shared clubs, an upcoming driving test, or even the same sense of style. Personal style is an important part of identity in high school, one that most students think about daily. It can be an obvious way to find classmates with similar interests.

Peer pressure is when members of a group influence individuals to engage in certain behaviors or act in a particular way. Many high schoolers feel like they need to find a social circle to fit in, but this can lead some people to choose the wrong friends. A healthy social group is built on mutual respect and companionship. If members disagree, they talk through their problems and find a solution that works for everyone without making anybody feel left out.

A toxic group, on the other hand, assigns more value to certain people. To stay in the circle, members need to prove themselves to the unofficial leaders. Due to this mindset, newcomers can experience intense pressure to conform and follow along with the rest of the group. It's a way of wanting to be accepted, but it can lead to bullying and other negative behaviors.

For example, imagine that you're a freshman at a new school. You get partnered with an existing group of friends in gym class. They're the first people to pay attention to you, so you're eager to be liked and fit in. When they start gossiping about others in the class, you join in and make mean jokes that you later feel guilty about. Even though they didn't tell you to make jokes, you were still influenced by being around them.

However, not all peer pressure is negative. Some instances of peer pressure influence you to behave in a healthier manner that builds positive traits. For example, if all your friends arrive at school early to study before important tests, you might join in because everyone else is doing it. You're still making decisions based on what others around you are doing, but the outcome is a positive one.

This positive peer pressure demonstrates that it isn't the pressure itself that's inherently bad. Instead, it's about who you choose to let into your life and whether your friends are a good influence. Similarly, you should also consider how you impact the people in your life and whether you're encouraging them to become better people with healthier habits.

# STRATEGIES FOR HANDLING PEER PRESSURE

A simple strategy for handling peer pressure is to concentrate on how the situation makes you feel. If you're uneasy or nervous, your gut might be telling you to think twice before you act. When a group or an individual person tries to push you beyond your comfort zone, consider which direction you're heading.

Healthy change can still be difficult and cause you to feel discomfort. This is why you need to dig deeper into your emotions. Ask yourself whether you're just facing growing pains from a positive decision or whether you're hesitant to do something because it goes against what you believe in. Taking a moment to work through your emotions prevents you from making knee-jerk reactions or giving in when others put on the pressure.

Another technique to respond to peer pressure is to set better boundaries with your friends and loved ones. Some people don't realize they're overstepping because they think they're giving you advice or sharing their opinions. Communicating that you're feeling pressured makes the other person aware of how they're acting. Once they understand there's a problem, they'll be more likely to pay attention to your feelings and respect your boundaries.

When you're faced with negative peer pressure, and the people you're associating with refuse to respect your feelings, it's probably time to break ties. Walking away from toxic relationships removes you from negative influences and situations. It also leaves more space in your life to find the people who truly care about you and won't pressure you to engage in harmful behaviors.

# RECOGNIZING AND RESPONDING TO BULLYING

Not all peer pressure escalates into bullying, but you should know how to recognize the signs in yourself and others. Bullying is when someone behaves aggressively or tries to intimidate another person. Not all instances of abuse are physical. Verbal teasing, hurtful jokes, and gossiping are less obvious forms of bullying.

In some cases, bullies make demands from the people they're targeting. They often ask for money or tell someone to do something embarrassing. The person who's being bullied might comply simply because they believe it will make the bullies leave them alone. Unfortunately, this is rarely the case. Bullies are motivated by the power they believe they have over others.

If someone is bullying you, it might seem like asking for help will only make the bully angry. Reaching out is a way to get other people on your side. When you balance the equation, and the bully realizes they aren't in control anymore, they're less likely to continue picking on you. Telling an adult about the bully also brings attention to the fact that they may have been hurting others as well.

A few signs that someone is being bullied may include changes in their behavior, mood swings, or physical injuries like bruises. If you think a friend or classmate is being bullied, consider talking to them to see if they need help. This can prevent any misunderstandings and clarify exactly what's going on. If you don't feel comfortable reaching out on your own, you can tell a teacher, counselor, or another adult.

You should never try to confront a bully on your own, as that could only make matters worse or put you in harm's way. Bullying isn't always physical or violent, but the situation could quickly escalate if you try to intervene.

## BUILDING CONFIDENCE AND SELF-ESTEEM

The right group of friends will be supportive and cheer for you as you work toward your goals. When they pressure you to think or behave a certain way, it's because they're pushing you in a positive direction. Instead of wanting to control or intimidate you, true friends want to see you succeed and grow into a happier person.

However, external support isn't a replacement for self-confidence or self-esteem. It's still important for you to be able to appreciate your own unique skills and contributions to the world around you. As silly as it might sound, you must try to connect with your inner self and who you really are. Understanding your own strengths, flaws, motivations, and fears will take time, but truly knowing yourself is an essential part of building self-esteem and self-love.

If you're struggling to find positive attributes about yourself, consider reaching out to a close friend or relative to share how you're feeling. Sometimes, a quick "pep talk" from someone else is all it takes to mentally reset and see the amazing traits that others already recognize in you. For example, if you're upset because you made a mistake in your solo during an orchestra concert, your friend might be able to rebuild your confidence by pointing out that you played every other section perfectly.

Many people also benefit from dressing up and looking their best. Pampering yourself in your free time can help you build confidence in your identity, style, and self-image. Putting on your favorite outfit, getting a haircut, or buying some new accessories can make you feel amazing because you love the way you look.

# CHAPTER EIGHT: PRIORITIZING MENTAL HEALTH

# RECOGNIZING SIGNS OF MENTAL HEALTH CHALLENGES

The signs that you're struggling with mental health challenges won't always look like what you've seen from your peers or on TV. For example, some of the most common misconceptions are that depression only makes you feel sad, and anxiety looks like a panic attack. However, mental health challenges can present with a range of physical and emotional symptoms.

Emotionally, poor mental health can make you feel sad, confused, or guilty without fully understanding why. You might be so worried about the future that you can't focus on anything else. This is especially true during periods of high stress, like applying to colleges or taking standardized tests.

Your moods might also be unpredictable or extreme. If you find yourself overreacting or lashing out at those around you, it could be a sign that you're having trouble managing your emotions. On the other hand, if you're feeling numb or emotionally disconnected from the world around you, that can also be cause for concern.

Mental health problems can also affect your physical wellness. It's easy to blame fatigue and low energy on a busy schedule, but if you're not feeling well-rested even after a good night's sleep, it could be a sign of a more significant issue. Other physical symptoms include loss of appetite, headaches, and unexplained pain. Keep an eye on how you're feeling to see whether you notice an improvement over time. If you feel stuck or like you're treading water after a negative event in your life, it's a good idea to reach out for additional support.

# STRATEGIES FOR MAINTAINING MENTAL HEALTH

Similarly to how eating a serving of vegetables won't magically make up for a terrible diet, there's no single technique that will suddenly improve your mental health. Often, people use multiple strategies to build mental wellness and cultivate healthy habits.

If part of your problem is overthinking, try going for a jog, cooking a meal, or playing a game. These types of activities occupy your immediate attention and make it harder to dwell on negative thoughts. You don't necessarily even have to try these strategies on your own. Inviting a friend or loved one to participate in a shared hobby can refocus your energy and make you feel less alone after a long day.

Plus, spending time around others gives you the chance to emotionally reconnect with the people who matter most in your life. Having fun with family, going out with friends, or having a deep conversation with someone you trust are all positive ways to boost your mood. You might not feel like doing anything when you first have the opportunity, but once you're more active and immersed in the present, it'll be easier to let go of whatever's weighing on your mind.

When you know you're about to face a challenging time, planning ahead makes a huge difference. If you have an important test to study for starting on Wednesday, schedule time for yourself on Tuesday. Find something you're really looking forward to and highlight it in your mind. A relaxing bath, a bowl of ice cream, and a movie marathon on Tuesday might be just what you need to prepare for the work ahead.

It's also a great idea to think up a reward for making it through a tough situation. Planning a fun weekend with your friends gives you a future milestone to get excited about. While you shouldn't go overboard and individually celebrate every task you complete, a small incentive can be incredibly motivating.

The key is to choose something you'll enjoy, no matter the outcome. If you only link your rewards to performance, you'll end up doubly disappointed if you fail a test *and* no longer feel like you're entitled to what you had planned.

# WHEN TO SEEK HELP

Everyone has days when they feel upset or out of sorts, and temporarily experiencing negative emotions isn't necessarily a sign that you need to seek help. High school can be a mentally challenging time in your life, and if you're busy with sports or handling a major project at school, it's natural to feel stressed out occasionally.

However, if you start to feel that your symptoms have gone on too long or they're disrupting your daily life, reach out to a trusted adult who can connect you with resources to help manage your emotions. Remember, mental health conditions don't always present in obvious ways. Some signs that you may need to seek additional support include the following:

- Trouble sleeping
- Inability to focus
- Loss of appetite or overeating
- Lack of interest in your favorite hobbies or activities
- Feeling disconnected from what's happening around you
- Thinking about hurting yourself or others

Mental illness is just as important to treat as physical illness. You should never attempt to solve ongoing symptoms by yourself or assume that they'll go away if you ignore them long enough. Even if you start by going to a family doctor you already know and trust, you're still taking that first step of telling another person that you're struggling.

## REMOVING THE STIGMA AROUND MENTAL HEALTH

In the past, it was less socially acceptable to talk about mental health. This is because many people viewed mental illnesses as personal problems rather than true medical conditions. Even though society has made progress by raising awareness of mental health conditions and offering more resources, it's still common for people to worry about how they'll be perceived if they ask for help.

An easy way to support your mental health is by educating yourself. Once you know more about conditions like depression and anxiety, you'll have the tools you need to speak up when you encounter harmful assumptions or outdated information. Many resources also include general recommendations about emotional wellness, self-care, and how to manage day-to-day challenges.

Being open about your own mental health can also encourage others to do the same. When your friends or family members see you discussing your own challenges and emotions, they may decide to share their own perspectives instead of attempting to hide their struggles. Even if someone in your life isn't ready to talk about their mental health, simply knowing you're there to support them can make all the difference.

A key part of being supportive of others' mental health is contributing towards a positive environment for all. Even a simple step, such as changing how you talk about mental health, can make a massive difference. Ableist terms, such as calling someone "psycho," only perpetuate the idea that mental illness is wrong, negative, or shameful.

# CHAPTER NINE: ACHIEVING ACADEMIC SUCCESS

# SETTING AND ACHIEVING GOALS

Like any other goals, your academic goals should align with where you are now and where you want to be in the future. Goals should follow the acronym "S.M.A.R.T.," which stands for specific, measurable, achievable, relevant, and time-bound. If you're too vague about what you want to accomplish or if you set the bar too high, you won't have enough detail to create a plan for success.

When you're setting a goal, think of how much time you need in order to accomplish it. Facing an urgent goal like getting your grades up can be daunting. Many people make the mistake of setting major goals that are so overwhelming that they don't know where to begin. When you're first starting out, it's better to divide a larger goal into smaller pieces that feel more manageable. Those early wins will build your confidence and momentum.

Instead of obsessing over your final grade for the entire year, concentrate on an upcoming quiz or a homework assignment. Once you see that you're moving in the right direction, you can broaden your focus to include larger increments of time, such as the whole marking period. Before you know it, you'll be well on your way to improving your final grade.

If you notice that your plan isn't working out as intended, don't feel down about yourself or abandon your goals. You might just need to make a few adjustments. Think about which part of your goal no longer seems attainable and what you can do to fix that. For example, if you're not able to study as much because you're in the school play, see if you can bring study materials to rehearsal to look over when it's not your turn on stage.

It never hurts to communicate with others to let them know when you're about to temporarily change your habits. When you need to dedicate all your time and attention to your academic goals, other things might need to shift. There's only so much time in a single day, and your goals for different parts of your life won't always fit together. This links back to prioritizing and understanding where you can let things slip for a little while.

If it's a choice between doing your chores or passing a test worth a huge part of your grade, then studying should obviously come first. Let your parents or guardians know what's going on, as they're likely to let you skip some chores or do them later if they know you need to concentrate on your academics.

Once you accomplish a goal, celebrate your achievements and reward yourself for all your hard work. Taking a break after you ace an important test allows you to reset after a challenge. If you're constantly moving from one goal to the next without any time off in between, you're putting yourself at risk of burning out.

# DEVELOPING A POSITIVE ATTITUDE TOWARD LEARNING

Learning doesn't stop when you finish high school. While you might not think school is relevant to the adult world, there are plenty of common skills that will carry over to your future career.

This realization can make it easier to develop an appreciation for learning since it's an activity you'll engage in for the rest of your life.

Figuring out which study habits work best for you is a key part of being prepared for the future. The study skills you use in high school will allow you to learn new things in the workplace with far less effort than starting from scratch. Learning quickly on the job can also help you make a positive first impression and develop competency faster than your peers.

Simply knowing how to learn in an efficient manner may even result in special opportunities. If your boss needs someone to take over a project at the last minute or learn the basics of a new language, they're more likely to think of you first if they know you can quickly absorb new information.

Additionally, being willing and able to learn will also help you adapt to ordinary changes in your daily life. Whether you're getting a new cell phone or memorizing the layout in a store, you're guaranteed to encounter situations where you need to remember new details or processes for later. Your future self will thank you for laying a strong foundation at an early age.

Developing an appreciation for learning should also extend to those around you. If you see someone struggling with something you know how to do, offer to teach them or show them a few tricks. Walking someone through a process not only facilitates their learning but also reminds them that they're capable of mastering new things.

# GETTING GOOD GRADES: TIPS AND TRICKS

Participating in class helps you learn because you are verbalizing key concepts with your teacher instead of depending on memorization or reading alone. When you engage with the material in new ways, you're more likely to make connections you might have missed by relying on one study technique. For example, singing a song about math might feel ridiculous, but if it helps a formula stick in your head, then it's worth playing along.

Another important element of success is taking good notes. High school hours can be long and demanding, but staying on task in the classroom will keep you from having to study as much later. Plus, you'll learn more from listening to your teachers than you will from attempting to read the textbook on your own. Your teachers are also more likely to highlight specific points that will appear on a quiz, test, or project.

Don't be afraid to ask questions if you're not sure what to do for an assignment. If the instructions don't make sense, reach out to your teacher to clarify them. Once you know what they have in mind, it'll be easier to make sure you meet those requirements. Some assignments will even include a grading rubric that describes the criteria for each grade, so make sure to pay close attention to them.

You should also consider the purpose of each assignment. If you need to write a poem in English class and put it on a decorative poster, the poem itself is likely to matter far more than the decorations. Many of these extra responsibilities won't have as much weight for your grade, so don't get too distracted by minor requirements.

If you're fortunate enough to have extra credit opportunities, take advantage of them whenever possible. Even if you currently have a stellar grade, it isn't guaranteed to stay that way. You never know when your grade might slip later in the marking period. A few extra credit points can give you a buffer in those situations.

It's also an option to ask for extra credit if your teacher doesn't offer it on their own. The worst they can say is no. If you've worked hard in class, turned in your homework, and participated on a regular basis, they're more likely to agree with your request because they can see that you're already putting in the effort.

## SEEKING EXTRA HELP: TUTORING AND ACADEMIC RESOURCES

Tutoring and other types of academic assistance are usually available through your school or local community. Common subjects such as math and English are easier to find tutors for, but it's possible to find tutors in other areas as well. If your school doesn't have what you're looking for, the library might be able to point you in the right direction. Your parents or guardians may also be able to find candidates by searching local community groups online or making a post on social media.

Budget matters when you're searching for private tutoring options. Paid tutoring can cost anywhere from $20 to $50 an hour, depending on the subject matter and the person's qualifications. College students tend to offer cheaper rates, and you may be able to find teachers who tutor in their usual subjects during the summer when they're off from school.

When you seek out extra help, pay attention to how you prefer to learn. Some people can absorb information by listening to the teacher talk in class, while others find it easier to read through a textbook and look at diagrams. The way you learn will affect what type of references work best for you. Academic resources don't always have to be through formal channels, such as school or a study group. Watching YouTube videos about core concepts or reading an online article can be just as effective.

The time of year may also play a role in how much help you need. You might be fine studying on your own during the school year, but if it feels impossible to remember any information after the summer, you could benefit from periodic tutoring during extended breaks. Meeting with a tutor for one day a week over the summer would allow you to practice skills, such as speaking a foreign language.

Furthermore, some students benefit from targeted study sessions for specific reasons, such as taking the SATs or ACT. Although many prep courses cost money, there are still free practice tests and study guides available online. Your high school might also host specialized tutoring sessions during or after school to help you prepare.

# CHAPTER TEN: PARTICIPATING IN EXTRACURRICULAR ACTIVITIES

# BENEFITS OF EXTRACURRICULAR ACTIVITIES

Extracurricular activities, such as sports, school clubs, and community groups, are a fantastic way to explore different hobbies and get involved. These activities allow you to participate in something fun while simultaneously developing teamwork and social skills. More importantly, you'll learn how to work together with a group, even though you might not be friends with everyone involved.

Learning to respectfully engage and collaborate with people you don't know or actively dislike is an important skill. When you get to college or start your career after graduation, you won't get to choose who you work with. You'll need to work through any miscommunications or personal differences in the workplace, so it's a good idea to start practicing now.

Luckily, when you join a group activity, you'll have the chance to meet similar people who have at least one shared interest. You might not get along with someone on your debate team, but if you both enjoy that club, you still have something to talk about. Remember that you don't need to be best friends if you can be civil and avoid letting your personal feelings negatively affect the whole team.

Extracurricular activities also look great on resumes and applications. If you're applying to a job that requires you to interact with the public, mentioning that you answer the phone while volunteering at an animal shelter shows that you have experience communicating with others.

For colleges, admissions personnel often like to see a range of different activities to show you're a well-rounded person. Therefore, if you already play a sport in the fall, you should consider seeking out something unique for the spring. After all, playing soccer and representing your class on the yearbook committee requires completely different skill sets.

Lastly, extracurricular activities are beneficial for your overall health and wellness. They allow you to stay connected to your peers and socialize with people outside your usual social circles. The people you meet through clubs and groups are part of your extended support network, and some of them may even become close friends over time.

# BALANCING SCHOOLWORK AND EXTRACURRICULARS

Setting a schedule can keep your priorities organized as you juggle schoolwork, extracurriculars, and your personal life. Many large tasks can be achieved in smaller steps to minimize how much time you need to spend on each in a single day. For example, you may need to decide how many pages you have to read each night to finish a book by next Friday.

Asking yourself questions like this on a routine basis will help you keep track of how you're spending your energy. Looking ahead to the following week ensures you can move things around as needed and adjust if you're unusually busy. It also enables you to communicate with others as early as possible and show respect for their time. If you accidentally scheduled a study session at the same time as your piano lesson, telling your teacher a week early is better than frantically calling a few hours before you're due to arrive.

While you're bound to run into scheduling conflicts occasionally, don't make a habit of pushing your obligations to the following day. By deviating from your plan, you can end up in a position where you won't be able to catch up. It's fine to skip your reading one night because you're exhausted, but if you put it off three nights in a row, you might end up having to spend an inordinate amount of time on homework to avoid blowing the final deadline.

If you're repeatedly running into problems, it's probably time to review how your schedule is structured. Let's say you plan on doing homework for 30 minutes every night during the week. However, when you try that schedule, you're too tired to focus on your extracurricular activities and the demands of the regular school day. As a result, you end up staying up late to get your homework done, and your original estimate of 30 minutes quickly turns into an hour.

Instead of accepting that you'll just have to slog through your work every evening, think about what you can do to make your studying more efficient. Taking a short nap when you get home from your extracurriculars could give you just enough of an energy boost to get through 30 minutes of studying and the rest of your evening routine. If that doesn't work, consider waking up early to study once you've had a good sleep.

In some cases, balancing schoolwork might involve quitting a team or an after-school club if you realize you overcommitted. It never feels good to back out after you've said you'd do something, but you also need to prioritize your mental health.

## CHOOSING THE RIGHT ACTIVITIES FOR YOU

The most important part of choosing an activity is ensuring it's something you enjoy. While you might want to join an activity to spend time with your friends, it's best to choose clubs that align with your own interests. Activities are a huge time commitment, and you might regret joining a team or group if your heart isn't really in it.

High schools often have dozens of different activities for students to try, but you'll have to investigate what's available at your specific school. Band, drama club, and sports are among the most common, but some schools also offer specialized activities like robotics. Joining clubs is usually easier at the start of the school year, but you might be able to get involved in a new activity mid-year by speaking to the faculty members running the group.

If you don't see anything you like, there's most likely a process to start your own club. You'll need to find a teacher to oversee it, and your school may require commitments from a certain number of potential members before your application is approved. Some clubs are part of a larger organization, so you'll need to submit information to the state or national level to form a new local chapter.

Unfortunately, not all schools have a broad selection of clubs and extracurriculars. If you're committed to trying a specific activity that isn't available through your school, there might be opportunities within your local community. Facebook groups and online forums have made it easier than ever to connect with others in your area. However, make sure any group you consider joining is appropriate for teenagers. When in doubt, ask a parent or guardian to help you with your search.

It's also perfectly okay to skip group activities altogether. If you prefer to practice singing in private lessons rather than joining a chorus, that's completely up to you. The important thing is that you're still engaging in an extracurricular activity and expanding beyond the regular subjects taught in school.

# LEADERSHIP OPPORTUNITIES IN SCHOOL

In general, jobs and colleges hope to see leadership experience on applications because it shows you are not afraid of responsibility. Athletes frequently demonstrate leadership by serving as team captains, and clubs often elect at least one person to lead their group. There are also school-wide positions, like class president and yearbook committee, that have leadership elements.

If you're intimidated by the thought of being in charge, leadership can take many different forms. Instead of being the spokesperson for a club, you could serve as the treasurer or fill another behind-the-scenes role. These supporting functions are essential, and holding an official position in a group still shows that you're putting in more work than a regular member.

Additionally, a leadership role doesn't need to be a year-round commitment. You could volunteer to take charge of a specific project if you don't have time for a permanent role. Running a bake sale to raise funds for your club or organizing a group event are both examples of taking charge and showing initiative.

There may also be leadership programs that you can attend over the summer. These types of programs are designed to build your personal development and teach you essential skills to serve in leadership positions. While some are sponsored by corporations to educate high schoolers about opportunities in a particular field like business, others have a wider focus on general leadership principles.

Furthermore, leadership is usually a major component of internships, even if their programs are focused on more specific subjects or topics. Global corporations like Lockheed Martin, Google, and Microsoft offer summer internships to help students explore opportunities in technical fields. Federal entities like NASA and the National Security Agency do the same.

If competing for a slot in a national-level program sounds too intimidating, see what's available in your local community. Chapters of the Boy Scouts, Girl Scouts, and Rotary International are spread all over the country, while other organizations may be limited to a single state or region. There are also remote volunteer opportunities where you can assist with digital tasks and other duties that don't require a physical presence.

# CHAPTER ELEVEN: EMBRACING INDIVIDUALITY AND DIVERSITY

# UNDERSTANDING AND RESPECTING DIFFERENCES

The world is a diverse and complex place, and learning to respect others' differences is a critical part of growing up. Not everyone will be like you or share your beliefs, cultural background, or values. However, this doesn't mean you should only seek out people who are like you, as that approach can limit your exposure to new ideas and your appreciation of society as a whole.

Everyone has some form of bias, no matter how hard they might try to remain neutral and see the world as clearly as possible. Biases can affect how you see certain people or groups, and it isn't always intentional. If you grow up hearing certain ideas from social media or the people around you, it might take time to understand how some of those ideas can be harmful to others or prejudiced against a particular group.

Learning to respect differences doesn't happen all at once. It's an ongoing process that takes time and effort. If you realize something you said or did was disrespectful, remember that lesson and try to do better in the future. Remember, keep an open mind and listen to feedback from others instead of just relying on your own assumptions.

Respecting someone's individuality also extends beyond core personal traits, such as their race or religion. Your classmate might have completely different hobbies, but appreciating who they are means accepting that they have their own interests. You don't need to enjoy the same things or see the world the same way to be respectful of others.

# THE IMPORTANCE OF INCLUSION

Inclusion is important because it makes space for people from all different walks of life. Being inclusive is about valuing differences rather than only paying attention to the majority. This type of mindset ensures everyone can participate equally and share their own beliefs without worrying about discrimination or harassment.

The next time you're planning an event at school or in your personal life, stop to think about whether you're being inclusive. If you're throwing a party for your entire neighborhood, is it fair to call it a Christmas party if not everyone celebrates Christmas? Small actions, such as using the right words, can make a huge difference in promoting diversity and making everyone feel welcome.

If someone corrects you or gives you advice about how to be more inclusive, don't take it as a personal attack. They're just trying to help you learn how to improve and be more accepting. You won't always know the right things to say or do, but once someone tells you, then you'll have the tools to be better next time.

Being inclusive can also lead to new friendships, insights, and perspectives. When people know you're welcoming and open-minded, they're more likely to share more about themselves when you're around. This can lead to interesting conversations you might not have otherwise prompted on your own.

The same idea applies to classroom environments. By contributing to an inclusive classroom, you're communicating to those around you that you want to hear their insights and perspectives. For example, someone who's unsure about sharing their thoughts might be more willing to participate if they know they won't face discrimination or biased comments.

# ADVOCATING FOR YOURSELF AND OTHERS

Unfortunately, not everywhere you go will be inclusive or accepting of individual differences. Some people maintain negative opinions about certain groups of people, personal traits, or lifestyle choices. If someone is deliberately going out of their way to discriminate against and exclude others, you won't always be able to change their mind.

Choose whether you want to intervene and advocate for a different point of view on a case-by-case basis. Pushing back when another person is set against you might only escalate the situation or put you in danger. As much as you might want to convince them to see your side, there are times when it's simply best to walk away.

The exception is if you're experiencing bias or harassment in places where it's illegal. For example, it's against the law for teachers in a school to discriminate based on religion, gender, race, sexual orientation, age, ability, or ethnicity. If you know this kind of behavior is taking place, tell a trusted adult what's going on and follow the official process to report a complaint.

As much as you might want to defend your friend and argue with a teacher if they do something discriminatory, making a formal complaint ensures your report is heard by the right people. It also protects you from retaliation if you're raising concerns about someone who controls your grade or has any other authority over your life.

Advocating for individuality makes it easier for people to express their true selves instead of being forced to follow along with the larger group. While critics often say that individualism makes people selfish, it can build independence and self-confidence. Being an individual is about appreciating your differences and standing up for your needs, preferences, and opinions. When you appreciate your own uniqueness, you're less likely to listen to negative influences or peer pressure.

## NURTURING YOUR UNIQUE INTERESTS AND PASSIONS

Part of acknowledging the value of individuality is nurturing your own interests. You won't necessarily enjoy the most popular activities, and others may even make fun of you for having hobbies that are "uncool." However, if they make you happy, other people's opinions of your favorite pastimes shouldn't matter.

You don't need to be the best at your hobbies to enjoy them. When you're first starting out and learning, you're guaranteed to make mistakes. No one picks up an instrument for the first time and instantly knows how to play the most advanced pieces. It takes practice and dedication to hone any skill, and you shouldn't let fear of looking bad keep you from pursuing your passions.

In fact, when you feel passionate about a particular activity, do your best to set aside time for it each week. You might not be able to spend hours on your hobbies when you have school, homework, or extracurriculars to think about, but you shouldn't ignore them completely. If you love cooking, choose one day to make a meal for your family. You can even work on more challenging recipes on the weekends when you have extra time to spare.

Even though you might feel insecure about your interests, it can also be beneficial to share them with others in your life. You never know when someone will have a suggestion about how to use your hobby in creative ways. Your parents or guardians may also seek out more opportunities for you if they know you're serious about a particular subject.

If your high school doesn't have any programs that relate to your interests, summer programs offered separately from the school system usually have a variety of activities. For example, wilderness camps show you how to survive out in the woods, while space programs will introduce you to the history of aeronautics. Some resources even have virtual options so that you can attend online from anywhere in the world.

# CHAPTER TWELVE: DEVELOPING LIFE SKILLS

# BASIC FINANCIAL LITERACY

Managing money is often stressful at any age, so developing financial literacy early in your life is a great way to build those skills over time. Even if you don't have a job or a regular source of income, it doesn't hurt to learn the basics of saving, spending, and investing. When you get money for your birthday or earn a few dollars doing chores, you'll know how to handle your money responsibly.

Techniques like stuffing envelopes with cash are popular on social media, but your money is also at risk of being stolen or damaged if you keep it around the house. A bank account gives you a secure place to store your money while also earning a little interest on what you've deposited. It's also a significant milestone in developing financial independence since you'll need a bank account to deposit paychecks and set up automatic bill pay.

Your parents or guardians may have already opened a bank account on your behalf. If not, you'll need their permission to open a new one unless you're already 18 years old. There are two main types of bank accounts: savings and checking. Some of these accounts have minimum deposit amounts, but many banks offer a free version with limited benefits.

A savings account pays more interest per year, but it limits how many withdrawals you can make on a regular basis. You'll receive an ATM card that allows you to take out cash from an ATM, but you won't be able to pay for purchases directly with that type of card. A checking account is designed for regular everyday spending, so that type of account will come with a debit card that you can swipe to make purchases.

Some people find it helpful to use a rule while saving money. The 50-20-30 rule states that you should spend 50% of your money on essentials, put 20% into savings, and spend 30% on things you want. However, this rule is also designed for adults who need to spend more money on needs like housing or car payments. If you don't pay for any of your own bills, you could adjust this rule to fit your habits and future needs.

For example, if you know you want to go to college, you could spend 30% on everyday expenses, put 50% towards your college fund, and deposit 20% into your account to save for something else you want. Talk to your parents or guardians if you need advice about the best way to break up your spending.

Many credit cards have monitored accounts designed for teens, and you would share it with your parents to learn more about how to use credit responsibly. Instead of withdrawing money right away, like with a debit card, a credit card extends you extra spending money. In return, you pay interest to the credit card company over time.

For instance, imagine that you want to buy a video game console for $500. You have $400 in the bank and a credit card with a limit of $300. Between your cash and the credit limit, you can buy the $500 item even though you don't have $500 in cash. When the bill comes for your credit card, you pay $100 toward the total. The credit card company then charges you interest on the remaining $200 you didn't pay off. As a result, you'll pay off more than $200 over time since you owe interest on top of the original amount left after your first payment. It's highly advised not to spend more than you can pay off all at once, as it is easy for your credit charges to get out of control and accumulate to a point where it's difficult to pay it off with the added interest rates.

If you don't have the option of getting a joint credit card with your parents or guardians, there are also secured credit cards that allow you to build your credit history with minimal risk to the bank. In this case, you deposit the amount of money required to cover your entire credit limit, and a financial institution issues you a credit card in return. This way, if you don't pay your bill, the bank already has the money needed to cover the debt since you deposited it when you opened the account.

After you show that you can reliably pay your secured credit card, the financial institution you're working with may offer you a conventional credit card where you don't need to pay the money upfront. Moving other types of bills into your name is another way to build up your credit history. When possible, sign up for automatic payments to make sure you never forget about paying your bills. Even a single negative mark on your credit history can have a significant impact at this early stage.

If you can't afford to sign up for autopay, consider asking your parents or guardians to make the initial payment on your behalf. You can pay them every month instead, and this way, if you accidentally miscalculate or have an unexpected expense, you're not in danger of missing a payment for your credit card.

# SELF-CARE AND INDEPENDENCE SKILLS

Self-care looks a little different for everyone based on your personal preferences and the things you enjoy. If you're an active person, then going for a jog to clear your mind after a long day can be an act of self-care. For others, taking a day off from exercise and sitting on the couch can be a time of much-needed rest. The important part is to choose a self-care regimen that improves your mental wellness without going overboard on indulgences.

Learning how to take care of your overall well-being is part of becoming more self-reliant and independent. As you get older, you'll have more control over where you go and what you do. However, that also means you'll be on your own for longer stretches of time, so you won't have people like your parents or guardians checking in with you as often.

Knowing your own limits is the key to setting boundaries and communicating with the people in your life. If you're already busy with schoolwork and your existing activities, it's totally fine to let others know that you can't take on anything else without getting overwhelmed. Not only does this protect your mental wellness, but it also establishes that you're capable of managing your own commitments.

If one of your goals is to become more independent, you may need to sit down with your parents or guardians to reestablish boundaries. For example, your parents might feel that you're not responsible enough to have a curfew as late as midnight, while you think you should be able to stay out as late as your friends because you're almost an adult.

You can also address some responsibilities you want to take over as you get older. The basic chores you should know how to do include cooking at least three meals, doing your own laundry, and knowing how to clean without damaging surfaces or objects. For example, some cleaning products are too harsh or unsafe in certain conditions, so tidying up can be far more complicated than it looks.

Additionally, you may want to take over responsibility for basic car maintenance. If you own a car or use a family vehicle, taking it in for oil changes and filling the tires with air will help you become more comfortable with these essential tasks. This way, you won't be so reliant on your parents or guardians if you realize that your car is due for maintenance.

Over time, you'll gradually start to take over more and more things as you grow older. Remember to take these steps slowly and gradually. If you attempt to tackle too many responsibilities at once, you're likely to become frustrated. If your parents or guardians are still handling some of your responsibilities, it might help to sit down together and create a plan.

It might make more sense for your mother to handle your health insurance since you're covered under the family plan she receives from work. In the meantime, you can learn more about how health insurance works and review your plan with your mother to better understand the specifics. While your mother is taking care of that aspect of your life, you could take over your cell phone bill or sign up for your own streaming services to increase how much you're contributing.

# COMMUNICATION AND CONFLICT RESOLUTION SKILLS

British cognitive neuroscientist and teen-brain researcher Sarah-Jayne Blakemore has called adolescence a "perfect storm" of challenges, with a host of changes to hormones, neural structure, and social relationships added to the increasing pressures of life. It's no surprise that this can lead to powerful emotions and increase the potential for conflict as you and your peers navigate high school.

Although it's usually a good idea to avoid conflict whenever possible, you'll inevitably have disagreements or arguments. Knowing how to resolve conflict in a healthy manner can keep you from saying things you don't mean or damaging your friendships in the long run. Once you recognize that you may be reacting to other influences besides the situation that caused the argument, you might realize that you're too tired or worn down to work through a disagreement at that moment.

In that case, it's important to communicate with your friend and say something like, "I don't want to argue, but I'm really upset right now. Can we talk about this tonight after I've had a chance to take a nap and reset?" This shows that you're still willing to talk things through at a later point, even though you've currently reached your mental or emotional limit.

Taking time to cool down can allow you to revisit the issue at hand with a clearer head. You might even find some relief in your ordinary pastimes, such as walking your dog, drawing in a sketchbook, or listening to music. Once you've settled a bit and had a chance to think about the situation, make sure you continue the conversation as you promised.

It's also valuable to know how to intervene in a conflict involving other people without causing the situation to escalate. Whether it's a bully targeting one of your classmates or two of your closest friends bickering over a misunderstanding, conflict resolution skills enable you to see potential solutions and choose the one that's least likely to end in a negative outcome. Frequently used conflict management techniques include the following:

**Avoidance:** Removing yourself or others from a conflict works best in situations where someone might be in danger. You should never try to argue or fight back in an aggressive encounter. Whether you find an adult to help or physically run away from the immediate area, the goal of this technique is to separate yourself from others involved in the conflict.

**Mediation:** Meditation is when you involve a neutral third party to hear both sides of a disagreement. If you get into an argument with your sibling, your parents or guardians might serve as mediators to talk through the situation. The goal of mediation is to resolve the conflict by discussing what happened and how each party feels about the situation.

**Compromising:** In a compromise, neither side is completely happy with the outcome. Instead, you give and take until you reach a solution that you both find acceptable. If you want to watch an action movie and your friend wants to watch a horror movie, a potential compromise would be to watch a comedy that you both enjoy.

**Active Listening:** Showing empathy and actively listening to the other party can clarify any miscommunications and ensure you're understanding their stance. People may be more willing to compromise if they see that you respect their thoughts and listen to their side of the story.

**Problem Solving:** If the underlying cause of a conflict hasn't yet been solved, working with the other party to fix the problem is likely to resolve it. For example, if you're angry with your sibling for eating the entire box of your favorite snack, you could work together to come up with a system of dividing snacks as soon as you get them from the grocery store. Making snack bins with an equal number of snacks for each person would solve the underlying issue and prevent the same conflict from happening in the future.

You don't need to use each of these techniques separately, as it isn't unusual to combine multiple methods while working through a conflict. If communication breaks down, try shifting to another technique or suggest a short break to cool off. Taking time to collect yourself and calm your emotions will keep you from lashing out or becoming too focused on "winning" the argument.

# DECISION MAKING AND PROBLEM-SOLVING SKILLS

High school is a somewhat unpredictable time in your life as you develop new routines and gain more independence. With graduation just around the corner, making even minor decisions can be surprisingly stressful. Being decisive is often seen as a positive trait, but you don't want to rush into choosing a particular path simply because your gut instinct tells you to go in that direction.

When you're faced with a decision, an effective technique is to consider the pros and cons of each choice. Fold a piece of paper in half or draw a line down the center. Use the left column for positives and the right column for negatives. This format makes it easier to visualize benefits and drawbacks all at the same time.

For example, if you're trying to decide whether you want to try out for the field hockey team, you might list physical fitness and camaraderie as positives. Meanwhile, the negatives might include losing free time in the evenings and having less energy to devote to schoolwork. Once you have both lists written out, you can compare the columns to see whether the positives of playing field hockey are worth the negatives.

You've probably had someone tell you to "sleep on it" when you're struggling with a problem, but that can be sound advice. Focusing on the same problem for too long makes you more likely to get frustrated and angry from mentally going around in circles. Getting some rest and starting with a fresh mind ensures you have your full brain power to dedicate to the problem.

Understanding how you learn can also help you find solutions. If you feel more comfortable seeing data as a graphic, draw a diagram with information about the problem. Writing down potential solutions is another approach to organizing your thoughts. You can quickly see what you've already tried and review any notes about what was or wasn't successful.

# CHAPTER THIRTEEN: PLANNING FOR THE FUTURE

# CAREER EXPLORATION AND PLANNING

There are hundreds of different careers you can explore as you prepare for the future. The first step in exploring a potential career is to determine the requirements for that role. Once you know the minimum amount of education or training involved, it will be easier to develop a long-term plan as you progress through high school.

While many paths lead to college, not all careers require a degree. It's up to you to decide whether college is a good fit for your personality and future goals. Plus, with the increasing use of remote education, you have flexibility in how you want to attend college if that's what you decide.

If you know you'll need strong math skills or physical fitness, you can adjust your high school schedule to prioritize those areas. Your career research is also likely to intersect with your search for colleges, internships, and training programs. Some of these may be available to you while you're in high school, allowing you to get a head start on your career. Your guidance office is an excellent resource if you need help looking up internships or summer programs in your intended field.

You may also be able to volunteer with or shadow someone who's already working in a career that interests you. This can help you understand more about the day-to-day life of working in those types of positions. If you want to be a veterinarian, volunteering at your local animal shelter on the weekends will allow you to interact with a variety of different animals and learn more about their health concerns. You may even get the chance to speak with veterinarians while at the shelter.

Don't get discouraged if you're still uncertain about what you want to do for a living; you don't need to have everything figured out. If you're approaching graduation and you're still not sure about a potential career, it doesn't hurt to take some time off to work or enroll in a few fundamental courses at the community college. You won't always know what you enjoy until you try it, and some people don't find their true passions until they're well into adulthood.

# COLLEGE PREPARATION: SAT, ACT, AND COLLEGE APPLICATIONS

Applying to college requires a substantial amount of preparation and forethought. Waiting until the last minute could jeopardize your chances of getting accepted to your top schools. Since colleges consider your entire high school career, it's wise to start thinking about what you'd like to study while you're still in your freshman year.

If you're one of the high schoolers who knows exactly where they want to go to college, you can schedule a tour or visit before it's time to apply. This way, you can see the campus in person and get a feel for the overall vibe of the school. Even if you've already visited before to see an older sibling or a friend, it's still a good idea to go on your own and meet with an admissions counselor. They'll be able to give you specific advice about applying and what you need to be successful if you're accepted.

College applications typically open on August 1, but you can start gathering the necessary materials over the summer. Deadlines are usually in January or February, but some college programs also offer early decisions if you submit your application by November. These deadlines matter less for schools with rolling admissions, where students apply throughout the year for the next closest semester. Colleges may also have different admissions processes based on whether you're applying for in-person sessions or remote learning.

In recent years, colleges have put less emphasis on admissions tests like the SAT and ACT. In some cases, it's entirely optional. Both the SAT and the ACT are timed, and you'll be allowed to use approved calculators on the math portion. On the day of your test, you'll report to a designated testing center to take the test in person with a proctor.

The SAT consists of three parts: math, reading, and writing. It costs $60 to sit for the SAT, but waivers are available if you can't afford the fee. The ACT is less popular but covers a broader range of subjects, including math, English, reading, science, and an optional writing section. It costs $68 for the basic ACT or $93 if you add on the writing portion.

Your scores on the SAT and ACT are only one part of the admissions process. You'll also need to complete an application, which usually includes writing an essay and filling in basic information about yourself. Since you've not finished high school yet, you'll send along an official transcript for all the courses you've completed thus far.

Many college applications also require letters of recommendation from teachers, coaches, or other adults in your life who aren't immediate family members. These letters should highlight your best qualities and most significant achievements. Remember to always give the person you're asking plenty of notice before writing a letter. Teachers and coaches receive dozens of requests, and it shows respect for their time if you let them know you'll need a letter of recommendation well in advance of the deadline.

When it's time to send in your materials, some colleges allow you to use the Common Application. This shared application saves you time since you can use the same information to apply to over 1,000 different institutions. However, you might still encounter a school on your list that has a separate application. Fees vary widely, but most applications cost between $50 to $60.

Application fees can quickly add up, so many students develop a shortlist of top schools with a few "safety schools" mixed in. Safety schools are usually less selective and have a higher rate of admission. Some of these schools might even offer free applications to entice students to apply. However, you should try to apply to approximately five to eight schools. If you're targeting extremely competitive institutions or Ivy League universities, you should have a higher number of safety schools to compensate.

In addition to standardized testing and your written application, most colleges will look at your disciplinary record. A day of detention might not seem like a big deal to you, but it could make an admissions officer hesitate if they're already on the fence about offering you a place in their incoming class. Try to avoid breaking any rules to the point that it goes on your permanent record.

# SCHOLARSHIPS AND FINANCIAL AID

Paying for college or other training programs is often a daunting prospect for potential students. College courses can range from several hundred dollars to thousands per class. Private universities are generally the most expensive, but you can significantly offset your college expenses by applying for scholarships and financial aid.

Scholarships are competitive, so you'll need to fill out an application, write an essay, film a video, or otherwise explain why you're the most deserving candidate. If essays aren't your forte, look online for lists of unusual scholarships. You might be pleasantly surprised by how many are available. There's even a scholarship for who can make the most impressive prom outfits using only duct tape!

Financial aid is slightly different. Academic institutions and educational programs may offer need-based assistance for students who have trouble affording the cost of tuition. The award amounts vary extensively based on the school and the cost. To qualify for financial aid, you and your parents will need to fill out the Free Application for Federal Student Aid (FAFSA) based on your household's income.

From there, colleges determine whether they want to award you scholarships, grants, or other financial assistance. The federal government may also offer you loans based on your application. You won't have to pay the interest that accrues on subsidized federal loans, but your unsubsidized federal loans will have interest that grows over time.

You may also qualify for private loans, but these types of loans typically come with higher interest rates than federal ones. Pay close attention to the repayment terms if you decide to take advantage of a private loan. Student loans can rapidly accrue interest, and it's not uncommon for graduates to still be making payments years after finishing their degrees.

Grants are ideal because you don't have to pay them back, and many of them can be renewed during all four years of your undergraduate education if you satisfy all of the requirements. For example, certain government grants, like the Pell Grant, help underprivileged students from low-income backgrounds attend college.

Once you're in school, you can work to offset the cost of textbooks, food, or other essentials. Some colleges and universities also offer opportunities to work in part-time positions during the school year. This can be a great way to get work experience in a low-pressure environment. Plus, since these positions are affiliated with the college, your supervisor is likely to be sympathetic if you need time off to study.

# VOCATIONAL PATHS: ALTERNATIVES TO COLLEGE

However, you don't need to go to college to have a successful career that pays well. Careers outside of a traditional college track usually have their own processes. Trades like plumbing and carpentry often have dedicated technical schools and instructional programs. Some high schools even have vocational programs where students can work toward trade certifications before graduation. You will spend part of the school day focusing on required core classes and the second half working towards licenses or certifications.

If you already know college isn't for you, start researching the career paths that are available without a degree. Some common occupations that don't require a college education include the following:

- Construction or building trades worker
- Truck driver
- Police officer
- Firefighter, EMT, or paramedic
- Hairdresser or cosmetologist
- Flight attendant
- Real estate agent
- Store or facilities manager
- Pilot
- Dental hygienist

This is far from an all-inclusive list. As you can see, some of the most interesting careers are attainable without a college degree. However, that doesn't mean you won't need to study and go through training before you can start in these roles. For example, a police officer must graduate from an academy before joining the force. A retail manager, meanwhile, is more likely to learn on the job or be promoted from within existing employees at the store.

In some cases, a degree is required to advance to higher positions. It can be beneficial to start working first before going to college if your future employer offers tuition assistance. You won't have to pay as much out of pocket, and your employer is more likely to be flexible about your class schedule if you discuss the program with them before you enroll.

Joining the military is another distinct track that follows its own process. You don't need a degree to enlist, but you will need one if you intend to join as an officer or become one later in your military career. The military encompasses the Coast Guard, the Navy, the Marine Corps, the Army, and the Air Force. Each branch has its own purpose, culture, and history.

To enlist in the military, you'll need to take the ASVAB, the Armed Services Vocational Aptitude Battery. The test is timed and measures your aptitude in different areas like science and math. Your scores allow recruiters to match you with different roles and opportunities based on each position's requirements. You'll also need to pass an in-depth physical exam to ensure you're healthy enough for military service.

Contract agreements vary significantly and include a host of different perks. You might be eligible for an enlistment bonus or repayment on existing student loans in exchange for serving a certain number of years. Active duty, which means you're serving in the military on a full-time basis, typically has more enlistment incentives. The other option is to serve part-time in the reserve.

Joining the military is a major decision that shouldn't be taken lightly. If you start an ordinary job and decide you don't like it, you can quit and search for something that's a better fit. With the military, you must satisfy your entire term of enlistment before you have the option to return to civilian life. Keep that in mind as you consider whether the military is right for you.

# CHAPTER FOURTEEN: GRADUATION AND BEYOND

# REFLECTING ON THE HIGH SCHOOL JOURNEY

Four years of high school sounds like a lot, but you'll be surprised at how quickly it speeds by. As you reflect on each year, think about what you've learned both inside and outside the classroom. Even if you had a tough year, focus on the bright spots and celebrate your perseverance during a difficult time.

Making a scrapbook to commemorate each year can help you remember all your favorite moments and experiences. If you have a close group of friends, you could work on it together as a group project. Print out pictures and add decorations to highlight major achievements and accomplishments. Your scrapbook can also serve as a supplement to your school yearbook, and they'll make wonderful keepsakes for after graduation.

Once it's time for high school to come to an end, think about the goals you set for yourself as you entered. If you couldn't complete them all, consider whether you can carry any forward with you as you move to the next stage of life. Even though you might not have met your goal on your original timeline, it doesn't mean you should give up on it completely.

For instance, if you really want to learn how to play an instrument, it isn't too late just because you won't have access to band or orchestra classes. A music store in your area will undoubtedly offer lessons, or you can even sign up with an online instructor for remote classes. Similarly, if you already have hobbies you enjoy, continuing with them as you move beyond graduation can be a bridge from one period in your life to the next.

You can also look back on any lessons you learned about how you study, collaborate with others, or manage your time. You can carry many of those skills forward with you as you enter the working world or enroll in your first semester of college. You don't have to repeat the same mistakes twice, so being aware of how you can improve can prevent those same issues from arising again.

# PREPARING FOR THE TRANSITION

As graduation grows closer, a little preparation can smooth your transition into the adult working world. You won't be able to anticipate every challenge, but you can tackle common concerns, such as finding a job and deciding how long you want to stay at home. Some of your timeline may be dictated by when college starts or how soon you anticipate finding a job.

If you plan to move away to college or pursue a career in a different state, you'll need a more in-depth plan that encompasses relocating to a new area. Moving into a dorm is a simpler process since the college will have points of contact to assist you with the logistics of moving in. Instead of having to pay for your room and board outright, you can use loans or other forms of financial aid as needed when you're living in student housing.

Finding a place to live independently of a college will be a little more demanding. You'll have to apply for a rental, show proof of income, and sign a lease. If you don't have a strong credit history that shows you reliably pay your bills, you might need someone else to cosign your lease. A cosigner is more established and guarantees to cover your bills if you're unable to pay for whatever reason.

It's also a good idea to share your plans with your loved ones. Explaining your vision of the future allows you to discuss potential issues and find solutions well in advance of when you graduate. You might think it's better for you to move out as soon as possible, but if your entire family disagrees, they may see other downsides that you haven't considered.

Don't hesitate to ask questions if you aren't sure what to do. No one expects you to figure out your post-graduation life on your own, and the people you know who've recently graduated will have insights that are relevant to the past. If you want to pursue a certain career or you're enrolling at a specific college, look online to see if there are forums, social media accounts, or blog posts about those exact paths.

Your journey after high school is entirely unique to you. You might want many of the same things as others you know, but your path won't be the same, no matter how closely you try to follow in their footsteps. Ultimately, you must find your own way, and that could involve taking a few detours as you figure out your goals for the future.

Finding the equivalent of a club as an adult can take some work, but the internet makes it easier to identify opportunities in your area. If you enjoyed drama club, see whether there's a community theater nearby with open auditions. In school, many of these points of connection are built in and facilitated by having so many people together every day in the same place.

As an adult, it'll take a bit more effort and creativity to find like-minded individuals. Many people make friends at work or in college, but since you will have more obligations, you won't all necessarily have the same schedules. Instead of planning to meet up during a defined lunch period in high school, you might need to plan social activities a few days in advance. It's an adjustment, but it'll soon be natural to work around what your friends and peers are doing.

When choosing friends as an adult, keep in mind the lessons from high school. Peer pressure still applies in adulthood, and bullies are inevitable as well. Since you have more freedom and independence, it can be easier to avoid these situations, but you still might run into an issue where people at work or college are trying to pressure you into acting a certain way.

As long as you're safe and happy, there's nothing wrong with living on your own terms. This includes the speed at which you try new things and step outside of your comfort zone. Some people can't wait to get their own apartment or move away to a different state, but that doesn't mean it's wrong to need more time to decide where or how you want to start your life after graduation.

Patience can also pay off. Instead of settling for the first job offer you receive, waiting to apply to only jobs you really want ensures you're starting your career somewhere that's most likely to be fulfilling. While it's fine to take a position temporarily just to pay the bills or get experience, it's even better if you find a job you are passionate about.

# EMBRACING CHANGE AND UNCERTAINTY

For the most part, high school follows a predictable schedule. You arrive and depart at the same time each day, and you know when to anticipate periodic breaks throughout the year. Furthermore, your high school friends are all on similar schedules, so it's simple to make plans and coordinate your social activities.

After graduation, your schedule will require a little more effort and attention. You might work different days each week or attend classes later than you did in high school. If your best friends have off at times that clash with your schedule, it'll take more coordination to meet up. Give yourself some grace while you figure out your new sense of normal.

You don't need to have your entire life mapped out by the time you graduate high school. Starting a full-time job, enrolling in college, or moving out on your own can feel overwhelming, but change is a normal part of growing up. Your friends will be facing many of the same challenges associated with this stage of your life, so you won't be alone as you search for the things that make you happy and fulfilled.

Bear in mind that the habits and techniques you use in high school won't always translate over to your post-graduation life. Your routines and needs are guaranteed to change as well. Instead of sticking to a set structure as part of your school day, it'll be up to you to make sure you're balancing work, family time, socializing, and other obligations. While the increased freedom and independence come with more uncertainty, every day can be different depending on how you choose to spend your time.

You'll also have more control over when you take time off to relax and reset. High schools have predetermined breaks throughout the year, but there's no rule that says you need to continue that pattern as an adult. Instead of spring break, you might prefer an extended holiday vacation or a trip with friends in the early fall. Unfortunately, you won't get summers off anymore unless you're working in education, but the upside is having a more balanced schedule throughout the entire calendar year.

The choices you make right after graduation aren't set in stone. For example, you might start taking one or two classes at the community college because you're not sure if college is right for you. In the meantime, you might also be working at a restaurant and saving up for a place of your own. After the first semester, you realize that college is much different than high school, but in a good way. You decide to enroll in more courses to finish your associate degree, but your long-term goal is to attend a four-year school and earn your bachelor's degree as well.

# LIFELONG LEARNING: CONTINUING TO GROW BEYOND HIGH SCHOOL

Regardless of whether you go to college or enroll in a training program, learning doesn't have to end when you graduate from high school. It's natural to want a break after the stress of final exams and finishing your senior year, but you shouldn't call it quits on learning altogether. There's so much left to learn beyond what you've encountered in high school, and you can now pick and choose the topics that interest you.

Even if all you do is read a news article in the morning while you have your coffee, you're still absorbing new information. In the past, people relied on physical newspapers and magazines, but digital alternatives make it easier than ever to read in snippets, study new subjects, or stay informed about current events. Something as simple as putting on an audiobook while you do chores or using a language-learning app on the train to work can keep your mind sharp for years to come.

Learning can take many different forms, and the everyday things you do for fun will likely require you to develop new skills. It's never too late to experiment with different hobbies or try something you've never experienced before. You might even discover a talent you never knew you had. From horseback riding to woodworking, there's no shortage of activities to keep you engaged in your free time.

Many people eventually decide to go to college when they're older, whether that's for an undergraduate degree, professional development, or a master's degree. A stable career and a balanced life might seem like a stronger foundation to launch an academic career compared to how you felt as a fresh graduate from high school.

Regardless of what you choose, the most important part is staying curious and making time to reflect on how far you've come. If you make a mistake, think of it as a learning opportunity and seek out ways to do better next time. Keeping an open mind and being receptive to feedback will ensure you're ready to listen when there's an opportunity to learn, grow, and ask questions.

# CONCLUSION

# LOOKING BACK, LOOKING AHEAD

High school is a major milestone in your life. Regardless of how much time passes, you'll still find yourself thinking back to high school, sharing stories with friends, or casually referencing your teenage years. Even if you aren't enjoying high school as much as you'd hoped, try to make the best of it by joining clubs, picking fun electives, or going to events.

You're almost guaranteed to have some regrets about your high school years, but if you realize you've made a mistake, there's still time to fix it. If learning Spanish is more difficult than you thought, think about whether you'd like to switch to another class when it's time to choose a new schedule next year. Don't let temporary disappointments keep you from appreciating the positives.

As you progress through high school, think about where you came from and where you're heading next. The past and the future can help you understand which choices to make in the present, but they can quickly become distractions. If you focus too much on what's to come, you might miss important moments that are happening around you now. Similarly, reviewing past missteps to avoid making the same mistakes twice is important if you aren't dwelling on the past. It's all about maintaining the right balance.

If the future seems scary, take heart from the fact that you've already made it this far. You were probably nervous about your first day of middle school, but you must have made it all the way through to reach this point. You've already accomplished so much, and high school is only the next stepping stone on the path to adulthood.

## EMBRACING YOUR UNIQUE JOURNEY

While your high school will inevitably have required classes and mandatory activities, you still have some control over your high school experience. There's no other point in your life that you'll have this much time and freedom to try new things. Take advantage of that by volunteering, playing a sport, or taking a class that's different from your usual interests. You'll never know whether you're a great public speaker or a whiz at dance if you don't try at least once.

Social pressures can also affect how you view various subjects and clubs, but anyone who makes fun of you because of your interests isn't a true friend. When people judge your decisions, that isn't a reflection of who you are or your value as an individual. You don't need to justify your friendships, hobbies, or career aspirations to anyone else.

Sure, your goal of moving to Hollywood and working your way up in the film industry might seem risky to your parents, guardians, or friends. However, if you have money saved up and a solid plan to follow your passions, the worst that happens is you give it a shot, and it doesn't work out. You might have to move home and regroup at some point, but you can be proud that you gave it your best effort.

Comparing yourself to what others are doing will only make you doubt yourself at a time when you should be concentrating on what makes you happy. You shouldn't outright ignore what your loved ones have to say; rather, remember that they aren't the ones living your life. If you're confident that you're on the right path, don't let others dissuade you from taking a chance on your dreams.

Luckily, once you figure out what you need to be successful in high school, those learnings will carry forward. Don't be afraid to step out of your comfort zone. Trying out for the soccer team as a freshman could end up with you becoming captain as a junior or a senior. Colleges might even offer you scholarships because of your athletics or the leadership you demonstrated as team captain.

Once you graduate, you'll already have a good idea of your interests and potential career choices. Even if you don't want to play soccer in college or on a local community team, you could end up working in a related field that involves sports. Your job as an athletic trainer or a sports journalist would then directly link back to the decision you made as a high school freshman.

# FINAL WORDS OF ENCOURAGEMENT

Reading this guide was a key step in preparing for the future and making sure you're ready for whatever comes your way. Whether you're about to start your first year of high school or you're an incoming senior, you now have all the tools you'll need to manage stress, build confidence, and know when to ask for help.

We also covered topics such as nurturing your individuality and engaging in self-care. The tips and techniques you learned in those sections will apply at any age. Growing up requires you to take on more responsibility, but that shouldn't mean sacrificing who you are or letting practical considerations overwhelm your well-being.

If you're feeling lost about what to do next, don't hesitate to come back and revisit some of your favorite sections in this book. Learning is a lifelong experience, and it can be reassuring to know that you always have a guide on your shelf to help you work through a difficult problem, form healthy relationships, or reconnect with your true self. Best of luck as you continue your journey through high school and into the greater world beyond!

Printed in Great Britain
by Amazon